CHRISTIAN DEVIATIONS

Christian Deviations:

THE CHALLENGE
OF THE NEW SPIRITUAL MOVEMENTS

A Revised Edition of
The Challenge of the Sects
by
HORTON DAVIES

THE WESTMINSTER PRESS
PHILADELPHIA

LIBRARY OF CONGRESS CATALOG CARD No. 65–21054

Published by The Westminster Press ®
Philadelphia, Pennsylvania

PRINTED IN THE UNITED STATES OF AMERICA

CONTENTS

PREFACE TO NEW EDITION

THE demand for a second revision of *Christian Deviations* provides the opportunity for third thoughts on a highly controversial subject. These afterthoughts have been provoked by my closer acquaintance with representatives of some of the new movements. It has been my privilege to instruct (and be instructed by) graduate students from some of them during a stay in California. As a result I am convinced that a dialogue is possible and highly desirable. Revisions have also been suggested by the often irate letters and generally cool book reviews I have received. For both criticisms, positive and negative, I am grateful and trust that the book shows their benefit. But, of course, the proof of the pudding is the eating. In this case, it is not the same mixture as before, and whether it is more palatable depends on the taste (and tradition) of the reader.

The most important new ingredient will be found in an additional and concluding chapter, *Epilogue: The Way of Encounter*, in which I argue for and exemplify (as I hope) a more eirenic approach between representatives of the historic churches and of the new movements. While doctrinal differences are important, yet no comity can ever be achieved by 'apostolic blows and knocks'. This is not to suggest that a tiger has become a dove, but perhaps he has developed vegetarian tendencies.

Anyhow, it seemed only right to erase references which were unintentionally offensive to representatives of the new movements. Where inaccuracies were discovered they have been corrected. I have tried to get up-to-date information on the new movements, especially recent statistics. This is harder than may be imagined, for some of them provide none, and others seem rather swollen. I have included useful statistics from *World Christian Handbook, 1962*, edited by H. Wakelin Coxill and Sir Kenneth Grubb, but in the absence of recent figures, or of any, the editors have often had to rely on educated guesses.

The title, *Christian Deviations*, is the best I can devise to cover a highly varied and selective group of new movements. They are exceedingly difficult to classify under one rubric. Theosophy is neither in intention nor in fact Christian, so it cannot be a *Christian* Deviation. Spiritism, although patronized by many members of the Christian churches, is not strictly a deviation so much as a supplement. Pentecostalism (in several of its associations) is clearly *Christian* in intention and in fact and has been welcomed into the Evangelical Alliance. The Seventh-Day Adventists, too, are almost as close to the historic Christian Churches, but their insistence upon the seventh day, and their unique doctrine of the Atonement, might allow them to be categorized fairly as Christian deviationists. Moral Re-armament was born in the mind of an evangelical Churchman, and was supported in its earliest days by many clergy and ministers, but in its latest years appears to have developed a moral ideology that supplants (although it claims to supplement) the work of the Churches. In turning away from its earlier inspiration, I believe that 'Christian Deviation' is a fair description. Christian Science, Mormonism and Jehovah's Witnesses, since all have added other special sources of 'revelation' to the Bible and, to that extent, modified its primary authority, are adequately covered by the present title. So, until I find a better term, I shall keep it. It will do no harm if it is realized that this book covers a whole spectrum of beliefs and practices that are Christian, semi-Christian and non-Christian.

The justification for bringing them together in one cover is that they show in our chaotic times some of the religious options, chiefly of recent growth, that confront men and women today.

The term 'deviations' requires me to define 'Christian' in both doctrinal and organizational fashion. For the former I am content to rest on either the Apostles' Creed as a convenient summary of belief or on the centrality of the Incarnation. For the latter I would claim that my terms 'historic Christian churches' or 'mainstream' Christianity are sufficiently intelligible references to the Roman Catholic Church, the Orthodox Church, the Anglican Communion, and the Protestant Churches, granting that the first two are more 'historic' than the rest. With the large exceptions of the Southern Baptists and the Lutheran Church-Missouri Synod who believe that their witness would be compromised by association with the Ecumenical Movement (and several of their ministers and laymen think otherwise), all these Churches consider that Christian divisions are 'unhappy'. Orthodox, Anglican and most Protestant Churches are vigorously participating members of the World Council of Churches, and they appointed observer delegates for the Second Vatican Council in Rome. These Churches (whether their members be conservative or liberal in theological outlook) give a primary place to the Bible as the record of God's revelation to old and new Israel, whereby he encounters and renews his people, making it the chief source of their beliefs, their worship, and their ethics. Each gives a subordinate place to tradition (though its strength and authority varies from Communion to Communion), which it interprets as the guidance of the Holy Spirit to the Church through the centuries, and is reconsidering the role of tradition as in part a hindrance, in part a help. We are in the thick of a new Ecumenical Age. Today as never before our Lord's appeal to all his disciples to be one is being responded to with urgency.

The next stage in re-union must take place on the left-wing of the Ecumenical Movement, for sufficient attention is already being given to the right-wing. 'Side-stream' Christianity must be brought into 'Mainstream' Christianity.

This study will have utterly failed unless it shows that there are deep social factors which create suspicion and hamper re-union as much as theological factors. Dogmatic authoritarianism or snobbish patronage can do incalculable harm to the delicate relations between separated brethren on each side of the divide. What is called for now is dialogue with honesty and compassion on both sides. It will demand patience and continuing involvement. It will shatter prejudices and stereotypes and be painful to the participants. But to this 'we' and 'they' are called and there will be an interchange not only of confessions but also of gifts and graces.

Department of Religion
Princeton University, Princeton
New Jersey, U.S.A.

1

THE CHALLENGE OF THE
NEW SPIRITUAL MOVEMENTS

*Be ready always to answer every man that asketh you
a reason of the hope that is in you . . .*

(I Peter 3.15)

IT IS a paradox that the present century, which has witnessed
the greatest growth of the Ecumenical Movement for the re-
union of the divided Christian Churches, has also seen the
fastest expansion of the sects and cults which split Christendom further apart. The 'great new fact of our time' (as Archbishop William Temple termed the Ecumenical Movement) is
counterbalanced by the great *old* fact of our time—the renewal
of heresy and schism.

So strong are some of these new movements that they can
no longer be regarded as harmless oddities and eccentric deviations from the historic norms of Christian faith, worship and
behaviour. Their very success in perpetuating error, strife and
bitterness constitutes their challenge and menace to the historic
Christian Churches.

Our concern in the present chapter is three-fold. It is, in the
first place, to recognize fully that the most Christian of these
deviations have demonstrated a remarkable growth in numbers, in the expansion of their missionary activities and in
the most modern means of propaganda, in recent decades.
Secondly, we shall consider the confusion caused by sectarian
Christianity on the mission-field and its betrayal of Christ's
will for unity among his disciples. Thirdly, an attempt will
be made to account for the dynamic appeal of the sects, not
in terms of their doctrinal deviations, for this will be the concern of Chapter 11, but from the standpoint of their social

cohesiveness, their simple authoritarianism, their emotional warmth and similar factors.

I

All the available statistics go to show that the sects are experiencing a phenomenal rise in membership. It will be well to begin with the sect that is most widely committed to missionary activity—the Mormons, or, to give them their official title, the Church of Jesus Christ of Latter-Day Saints. As if to mark the gauntlet which this American cult has thrown down to the stable and religiously conservative British people, the Mormons have recently built a vast modern temple in the metropolis, across the road from London's intellectual hub and mind, the South Kensington Science Museum. This new building, with its gold-leaved spirelet, is a powerful symbol of aggressive sectarianism. In 1962 there were 93 churches and an estimated community of over 11,000.[1] The Mormon leaders told one observer that 50 new churches were planned in Britain in three years.[2]

The success of Mormonism is almost entirely due to its marvellous missionary organization. World membership in this religious community now numbers 1,700,000 souls. It has over 10,000 missionaries in the field and it expects to gain many more missionaries in the near future. Fifty per cent of the members in good standing and in good health are expected to venture on a two-year missionary journey, often at their own expense for travel and maintenance, to whatever part of the world they may be sent from the headquarters at Salt Lake City, Utah. He or she may go to South Africa, to Switzerland, or even New Zealand. This is, indeed, a most vigorous expression of the Protestant principle of the priesthood of all believers. Often these missionaries are in the very prime of health and strength and their candid, outgoing personalities make a great impression because of zeal and radiant integrity of life. Is it, then, surprising that these young Mormon ambassadors are partly responsible for a 30 per cent increase in Mormon membership in the last ten years?

[1] *World Christian Handbook*, 1962, p. 209.
[2] See Geoffrey Moorhouse's article, 'Mormons in Britain', *The Manchester Guardian Weekly*, March 2, 1962, p. 12.

The rate of growth of the Seventh Day Adventists is even more striking. In 1950 its membership (Adventism's) was given as 225,000. In 1960 it was 305,000. The rate of increase was 36 per cent.[1]

The statistics of the Spiritualists in the United States also show a remarkable increase. In 1950 they claimed 126,000 members. In 1960 their members were estimated at 175,000. This represented a rate of growth of 44 per cent.[2]

The most active proselytizers among the sects are the Jehovah's Witnesses, who believe that all governments and all the Christian Churches are in abysmal error. The world-wide figure of their membership in 1951 was about 440,000. By means of a mammoth publishing programme, radio propaganda, and an army of tract-sellers with the pertinacity of successful commercial travellers who make frequent 'back-calls', they are the best-known, if not the best-liked, of all the sects in the English-speaking world. They well deserve the appellation of aggressive missionaries. It is known for certain that in the decade from 1942 to 1952 their numbers doubled in North America, multiplied fifteen times in South America, twelve times in the Atlantic islands, five times in Asia, seven times in Europe and Africa, and six times in the Pacific islands. Their leading publication, *The Watchtower*, has grown from an initial circulation of 6,000 copies in 1879 to over three million copies per month in 1960. It is no less significant that *The Watchtower* is published in 46 different languages.[3]

It should already be clear that the astronomical recent growth of these and other sects and the dissemination of their views by enthusiastic missionaries and through the medium of the radio and the printed page, constitute a serious challenge to the Christian Church. If their work were only among the pagans or the uncommitted of the modern world, then concern for their success might rightly be interpreted as a dog-in-the-manger attitude. The great danger, however, comes from the arrogant dogmatism with which most of them claim that they

[1] Statistics obtained from *Christianity Today*, vol. 6. December 19, 1960, p. 3.
[2] Statistics obtained from *Christianity Today*, vol. 6, December 19, 1960, p. 3.
[3] *Ibid.*, p. 21.

alone have the full and untainted truth and from their often successful attempts to steal sheep from other folds of the Christian Church.

Moreover, for anyone who takes seriously to heart the High-Priestly Prayer of our Lord that 'they may all be one', the sight of ever-increasing fragmentation of Christendom is intolerable. Our Lord, as recorded by the Fourth Evangelist, evidently wished his Beloved Community, the Church, to manifest the divine love on earth which characterized his own relationship with the Father, 'so that the world may believe'. The root objection to sectarianism is that it provides for a world already split into suspicious political, racial and social camps, not the secret of a supernatural unity, but the competition of the arrogant and the vindictive. Thus, his life and sacred Passion, which had as its aim reconciliation and atonement, is betrayed by a Christendom not at one, but at odds. Therefore, indeed, the world will not believe. The denominations have been at fault, and the new movements have splintered the witness even further.

II

The bewilderment and confusion caused by competitive sects is strikingly illustrated from both the sending and the receiving countries on the mission-field.

Bishop Azariah of India once pleaded at an ecumenical conference that the European Churches should cease to introduce into India sixteenth and seventeenth century differences of Protestant doctrinal emphasis (Calvinist or Arminian) and of Church government (Episcopalian, Presbyterian and Congregational), as they were increasingly irrelevant in Europe, and wholly irrelevant in India. He made the further point that there was no justification in calling out Hindus from a religious caste-system only to place them in a Christian denominational caste-system. The point, with reference to the vast land of China, was wittily put by the missionary who asked: What have the Southern Baptists to do with the Northern Chinese?

A personal experience of the writer, while living in the Union of South Africa, may be apposite here. He found that three different groups of African Congregationalists were under the impression that they belonged to three separate denominations. One group described themselves as 'C.U.S.A.' Christians; another group called themselves 'L.M.S.' Christians; while a third group wished to be known as 'A.B.C.F.M.' Christians. The interpretation of this rash of initials meant that the first group had been evangelized by the Congregational Union of South Africa, an indigenous South African expression of Congregationalism. The second group were the converts of the British London Missionary Society. The third group were the members of the flock of the American Board of Commissioners for Foreign Missions, with headquarters in Boston, Massachusetts. Confusion could hardly be more complete! What makes so untimely the further confusion of the sects is that the newly emerging Africa, with its several autonomous Republics, has so often confused essential Christianity with its European trappings and American overclothes, not to mention the association with a white racial superiority (less often expressed by missionaries than by other settlers, let it be said!), that they may be tempted to reject Christianity altogether as incompatible with a virile independency.

In the South African Republic the government officially recognizes over a thousand different sects! Thus African tribalism has repaid the confusion with which competing denominations and competitive sects have disseminated their tenets. It is extraordinarily difficult for the most perceptive African (and European, for that matter) to disentangle essential Christianity from the cultural envelopes in which it is enclosed, when he receives the Christian faith and worship from Polish Roman Catholics, Swedish Lutherans, Anglican High Churchmen, American Congregationalists, British Methodists, Afrikaners of the Apostolic Church Mission, and from Presbyterians who are British, Dutch and French, to take but a few notable examples from South Africa. How much greater, then, is the confusion caused to those taking their first halting steps in the Christian way when the sects make confusion worse confounded! It is not merely embarrassing or inconvenient, it is a scandal—a tearing of the seamless robe of Christ at a time when the historic Christian Churches are deeply penitent for their 'unhappy divisions'.

It is, perhaps, of unusual interest that most of the groups which will be considered in the following pages first took their rise in the United States of America. This is true of Christian Science, with its headquarters in Boston, Massachusetts; of the largest Pentecostal body, the Assemblies of God, with headquarters at Springfield, Missouri; of the Seventh-Day Adventists, with headquarters in Washington, D.C.; of the Mormons, with headquarters in Salt Lake City, Utah; of the Jehovah's Witnesses, with headquarters in Brooklyn, New York State; of the National Spiritualist Association, with headquarters in Milwaukee, Wisconsin; and it is also true of Moral Re-armament which was founded by an American Lutheran, Frank Buchman.

The fact that so many groups originated in the United States is occasionally attributed by the unthinking to the inherent viciousness of the American temperament, and often by persons who accuse Americans in the same breath of a deplorable tendency to social conformity. The deeper reasons for the vigorous variety of denominations and sects in the United States are two. In the first place, when the United States first came into being as an independent nation (no longer an overseas colony of Britain), the founding fathers determined that there should be a complete separation of Church and State. No single established Church could have met the needs of the new nation, with Congregationalism predominant in New England, Presbyterianism in the Mid-Atlantic States, Anglicanism in Virginia and New York State, Quakerism in Pennsylvania, Roman Catholicism in Maryland, and significant groups of Lutherans, Methodists and Baptists elsewhere. In consequence no denomination was favoured and so each had to set vigorously about the task of raising its finances to pay its minister and to erect buildings suitable for worship and Christian education. An aggressive missionary spirit is therefore characteristic of American Protestantism and Catholicism, as is a plurality of denominations and groups accorded equal status before the law.

The second factor accounting for the spread of new cults was the remarkable extension of the Westward-moving frontier in the nineteenth century. Here the rugged individuals who pioneered the new trails through the mid-West to the coast of California would not be content with the traditional and staid church ways of the Eastern seaboard. They desired and obtained a more spontaneous expression of religion, such as the camp-meeting revivalists provided, a faith in which they co-operated with God for their salvation, and a form of church government in which they managed their own church affairs without dictation from hierarchy or connexion. New prophets, like Joseph Smith the Mormon leader, or William Miller, the Adventist founder, found in the optimistic and millennial atmosphere a ready hearing for an indigenously American revelation or new interpretations of the old faith.

If, however, Americans planted the largest crop of new groups, it should not be forgotten that they have also been deeply concerned for the reintegration of a split Christendom. It should be recalled that the famous Lambeth Quadrilateral of 1920, which formulated the basis on which the Anglican Bridge-Church was prepared to welcome unity with other Protestant Communions without sacrificing its Catholic heritage of the Ecumenical Creeds and the three-fold and historic ministry, was only reiterating proposals that American Episcopalians had formulated in Chicago several decades before. Huntingdon, Bishop Brent and John R. Mott are as important names in the Ecumenical roll of fame, as are Archbishop William Temple, Bishop George Bell, and Archbishop Nathan Soderblom on the other side of the Atlantic. Furthermore, in the study of the non-theological factors that have promoted separation among the Churches, Professor H. Richard Niebuhr's *The Social Sources of Denominationalism* is as penetrating a study of the modern period as Professor S. L. Greenslade's *Schism in the Early Church* is of the period of the Church Fathers. Moreover, there have been important mergers of separate Churches in the United States to give proof that there is a strong will to Ecumenism in that vast country.

III

The growth of the new groups has been described as 'the unpaid bill of the Churches'. This epigram may be interpreted as meaning that these groups exist to stress those doctrinal elements or practices which the historic Churches have neglected or ignored. That this is a centrally important factor in accounting for the rise of the new groups will be argued in chapter 11 of this book. The epigram is also true in another sense: that is, that various non-doctrinal factors of a social and cultural nature are also responsible for the rise of the groups and it is to an examination of these sociological factors that we now turn.

It is undeniable that many groups, and even denominations, come into being simply because the existing Churches or denominations have lost their early fervour and become strongholds of the respectable and circumspect middle classes. These new groups or denominations, therefore, show all the characteristics of 'churches of the disinherited' (as H. Richard Niebuhr terms them). They are consciously established as the refuges of the poor. The Baptists, the Quakers and the Methodists began in this way. As their members rose in the economic scale, became more cultured and began to compromise their original world-renouncing ethics, those left behind in the social struggle drew apart into separate and congenial groupings. It is such folk who constitute the main support of the contemporary cults, such as the Pentecostalists, the Seventh-Day Adventists, and the Jehovah's Witnesses, although prosperity is improving the social status of the first two groups. Royston Pike says of the Jehovah's Witnesses that

> The heaven that is preached in Kingdom Hall is the sort of place that may well appeal to the man who knows what unemployment means, who has had to tighten his belt, who works at a monotonous job, who has tried to bring up his family in a smelly little box of a place. It is the sort of place that will appeal to the woman who has had to share a kitchen and has had too many children when she didn't want them, and had to nurse a girl with polio or mourn a baby that hardly lived to breathe.[1]

This is the religion of the hard-pressed and frustrated, who, without such faith and the company of their fellows at the bottom of the social scale, would be the utterly defeated. Suspicious of an educated ministry, or formal ritual and ceremonial, they find the greatest satisfaction in the emotional freedom, the naïve supernaturalism, the vivid personal ser-

[1] *Jehovah's Witnesses* (Philosophical Library, New York, 1954), p. 135.

mons with crude rhetorical devices, and the democratic forms of church government, which the parent denominations have outgrown. It is also significant that they exalt the simple manners, necessitated by their indigence, into moral virtues.[1] Honesty, thrift, abstinence, simplicity, diligence—these reflect their economic position almost as much as their moral ideals.

It is also significant that it is among such groups that millennial ideas have spread. These are, indeed, the defence-mechanism of the disinherited. The reward for poverty in time is an eternity spent walking on golden streets. Despairing of obtaining substantial advantages from the usual and all-too-gradual social processes, they reject the world that first rejected them, and they eagerly await the cosmic cataclysm that will cast down the mighty from their seats and exalt the humble and meek. In consequence, the leaders of the sects laud the God who is 'the Help of the helpless', while the leaders of the longer established Churches seem to serve a God who 'helps those who help themselves'. The ultimate vindication of the 'saints' is, for the sects, the thousand years of the rule of Christ preceded by Armageddon; for the members of the *bourgeois* and comfortable denominations the vindication of religious faith is the establishment of religion as a way of life that will promote greater brotherhood among men and the elimination of social tensions. As the sectarians look beyond time for entry into the Kingdom of Heaven, so do the historic denominations await a Kingdom of God upon earth. As their eschatological ideas differ, so do their conceptions of God. For the sects God is conceived in transcendent, irruptionist manner, 'terrible as an army with banners', the God of hosts, terrible in wrath to the worldlings, but inexpressibly gracious to his elect. For the denominations, God is conceived as an indwelling Deity, whose will is gradually fulfilled in the processes of nature and society, at the promptings of benevolence.

Sectarianism has its own distinctive code of ethics, as we have hinted already, and this is a corollary of its worldly estate. It is a legalistic, rigid, Puritan, black-and-white morality which divides men and women all too easily into world-affirming goats and world-renouncing sheep, or, in other words, into

[1] See Elmer T. Clark, *The Small Sects in America* (revised edn., Abingdon Press, New York and Nashville, 1937), pp. 219ff.

children of darkness and children of light. The vices are merely the practices of the opulent. Hence the sectarians ban such worldly amusements as dancing, cinema and theatregoing, the use of tobacco and of alcoholic drinks. They despise all ostentation and all literature, art and music that is not propaganda for their particular tenets, as wholly mundane. On the positive side, austerity of life, self-denial in things naturally desired, abstinence and mortification of the flesh, are the moral foundations of their code. There is, indeed, an attractive, if spurious, simplicity and exhilaration in the world-renouncing ethics of the sectarians, and it provides their communities with a firm cohesion and unity. Nonetheless, it is a naïve simplicity, for the world cannot be divided so conveniently into sinners and saints, since both cohabit in the same person. Moreover, sectarianism has its own subtle temptations to pride and uncharitableness. For this reason a transformist ethic, for all its agonies of decision made in the twilight of imperfect choices and inevitable compromises, seems preferable to a fugitive ethics of renunciation.

If the *bourgeois* complacency of many of the existing denominations has made the members of the sects feel unwelcome, they also make them feel emotionally starved. For members of the historic denominations, whose education makes them more emotionally restrained, rare attempts are made by the festivals of the Christian Year, 'Dedication Sundays' or such devices, to renew a sense of the great convictions that transform men from the top of the mind to the bottom of the heart. On the whole, however, the comfortable find emotional outlets in cultural associations and social recreations usually outside the churches. For the sectarians, however, religious community provides the whole of their life. Indeed, the sectarians deliberately adopt devices to stir up the emotions and, with complete sincerity, they attribute the results to the direct activity of God, the Holy Spirit.

The perfectionist sects, in particular, seem to insist that an emotional reaction is the only *proof* that the individual soul has made direct contact with God. Christianity for them becomes a religion of feeling. For this reason they particularly covet 'blessings'—gifts and outpourings of the Holy Spirit, *charismata*. In an ascending series they long for the experiences, first, of conversion and forgiveness, next of holiness or the 'second blessing', which gives an inner sense of complete purgation and harmony with the will of God, and, thirdly, the gift of tongues, visions, prophecies, which correspond to the mystical state of 'spiritual marriage'. In consequence, they prefer a simpler, spontaneous, highly-charged emotional service to the use of any liturgy. Their hymns are sung to urgent, staccato rhythms and tunes that are as easily memorized as the simple words, with their repeated choruses. The prayers are highly personal and extemporary, and they are often punctuated by the fervent cries of 'Hallelujah' and 'Amen'. The preaching is also extemporary and frequently crudely rhetorical in character, with passionate denunciations of the worldly, tender appeals to accept Christ as Saviour, horrific accounts of Hell or the more-likely-to-be-realized eschatology of the Hydrogen Bomb, and simple testimonies to the protecting power of God. The appeal is rarely to the reason, almost always to the emotions.

Another characteristic of the sects is their craving for objectivity and authority. The members seem to demand of their leaders that they give them certainties, since they have enough doubts of their own. As they find the black-and-white ethical code a respite from the responsibility of weighing motives, intentions and results, so they cannot bear the burden of thinking out the Christian faith anew in the light of modern thought. They are conservative biblical literalists in most articles of belief and they appear to believe that all persons must think alike. Utterly suspicious of tradition, they would eliminate all the centuries of Christian thought and experience between the first and the present as a prolonged era of apostasy. They believe it to be their duty to reproduce the Primitive Church in all its fullness as described in the pages of the New Testament. This attitude follows inevitably from their belief that the Bible is the infallibly inspired Word of God and that it contains the Christian faith, including all details of organization and administration which have been 'once for all delivered to the saints'. Allied to this conviction that they constitute the only true Church of Christ, however small their numbers, is the bitter necessity to condemn all other Christians.

We have already indicated how class distinction within the

historic Christian Churches, allied to a *bourgeois* complacency. has frozen out the perfervid sectarians. An equally important factor in promoting divisiveness and sectarianism has been racial exclusiveness, especially in countries where there are ethnic minorities. Professor Bengt Sundkler has shown in fascinating detail in his *Bantu Prophets in South Africa* how the indigenous African cults, as offshoots of Christianity, have arisen as protests against the arrogance of the white man. Sometimes they have taken the form of mating African nationalism with Christianity; at other times they manifest an extreme other-worldliness in which eternity is the compensation for a lowly status in time; at yet other times they include much African tribal lore and corybantic customs which the staid faith of the missionaries condemns.[1] Similarly, Professor H. Richard Niebuhr shows in *The Social Sources of Denominationalism* that Negro cults and denominations come into being to protest against their members being accommodated in separate parts of the white church where their supposed superiors seem to worship a white tribal Deity, or in order to have their more charismatic and emotional type of worship and to perform the duties and responsibilities of governing themselves in States where they were not allowed to exercise any civic responsibilities.

Perhaps the most pathetic example of the failure of the dominant white Christians in fellowship being responsible for the establishment of a Negro cult is to be found in the Coloured church named, 'The Church of the Living God, Christian Workers for Fellowship'. Its leader, Mrs Ethel Christian, claimed that she could prove from Scripture that Jesus was a Negro.[2] Arguing that Christ was the Son of David, and David the author of the Psalms, she claimed that the 119th Psalm proved her point. For there the Psalmist declares, 'I am become like a bottle in the smoke'. It is more relevant to lament the prejudice of the white Christians than to deplore the oddities of Negro exegesis.

---

[1] For a study of other 'independent' churches, see F. B. Welbourn, *East African Rebels* (SCM Press, 1961), C. G. Baëta, *Prophetism in Ghana* (SCM Press, 1962), Victor Hayward, *African Independent Church Movements* (Edinburgh House Press, 1964).

[2] Elmer T. Clark, *op. cit.*, p. 225.

IV

If the analysis of the part played by sociological factors in the acceleration of sectarianism is at all valid, then its meaning for the historic Christian Churches is readily seen. It is surely most important to recognize that the historic Christian Churches have been in considerable part responsible for the various revulsions that brought the sects into being. It is equally important to recognize that not all the blame can be laid at the feet of the denominations, for often the leaders of sectarian groups have been excluded by religious discipline from the historic Churches; sometimes they have been men of greater personal ambition and greed for power than men of spiritual vision. But the charge has sufficient relevance to make it imperative for the Christian Church to become in reality what it is in principle, the inclusive and Beloved Community. Dante saw inscribed over the portals of Hell the words, 'Abandon hope, all ye who enter here'. The Christian should see in his mind's eye, as he enters the portal of every Christian Church, the legend, 'Abandon all distinctions, ye who enter here'. Then the Church of Christ would be in fact what St Paul maintained it was in principle, one where 'there shall be neither Jew nor Greek, neither bond nor free, neither male nor female, but all one man in Christ Jesus'. A Church which perpetuates, instead of transcending, worldly divisions is already guilty of segregating and therefore of its own type of sectarianism, and is, of course, a great instigator of sectarianism.

If the Churches by their racial or class prejudices have become enclaves of arrogance or complacency, then they must bear the blame for the alienation of the under-privileged which resulted in the formation of sects as communities for the poor and disinherited. The cure for arrogance is that humility which comes from the common recognition that all men stand in need of forgiveness and the condition for receiving God's forgiveness is that we exercise it towards others. The cure for race prejudice and class exclusiveness is both a Christian colour and class blindness and active dedication to the pursuit of social justice.

Again, if the historic Churches have diluted their doctrine with the waters of modernistic compromise, or, to vary the metaphor, if they have muffled the strong trumpet of revelation, which condemns before it consoles, so that it gives forth an uncertain sound, they are to be blamed if sects come into being to bear more faithful witness to the biblical faith. The answer to this facet of the problem is for the Churches to rediscover the relevance and transforming power of the mighty acts of God culminating in the Incarnation, the Cross, the Resurrection and the Second Coming of the eternal Son of God, by which the life of the Church is renewed in the obedience of faith.

The Church is always in need of reformation. The challenge of the sects is therefore best interpreted constructively as a summons to reformation. If the Gospel is best commended by the Church as a community of supernatural charity which condemns the chill and forbidding respectability of this world, then the fanaticism and missionary aggressiveness of the sects, as also their fervent devotion to the person of Christ, is a goad to awaken the Church somnolent until it becomes again the Church militant. As John Wesley found that the essence of Christian communication was one loving heart setting another afire, the Churches must, in the final analysis, not only out-think but also out-love their opponents, the sectarians.

Even better would it be to avoid competition and to seek a genuine community of understanding at the grass roots level. At present there is too much isolation. As a result suspicion and misunderstanding of motives are rife.

Further reading

Atkins, Gaius Glenn, *Modern Religious Cults and Movements* (Allen and Unwin, London, and Fleming Revell, New York, 1923)

Black, James, *New Forms of the Old Faith* (Nelson, Edinburgh and London, 1948)

Braden, Charles S., *They Also Believe* (rev. edn., Macmillan Co., New York, 1960)

Clark, Elmer T., *The Small Sects of America* (rev. edn., Abingdon Press, New York & Nashville, 1937)

Gerstner, John, *The Theology of the Major Sects* (Baker, Grand Rapids, Michigan, 1960)

Greenslade. S. L., *Schism in the Early Church* (rev. edn., SCM Press, London, 1964)

Hoekema, Anthony, *The Four Major Cults* (Eerdmans, Grand Rapids, Michigan, 1963)

Irvine, W. C., *Heresies Exposed* (Pickering and Inglis, 8th edn., London, 1937)

Mathison, Richard, *Faiths, Cults and Sects of America, From Atheism to Zen* (Bobbs-Merrill Co., Indianapolis and New York, 1960)

Mead, Frank S., *Handbook of Denominations in the United States* (Abingdon Press, New York and Nashville, 1956)

Niebuhr, H. Richard, *The Social Sources of Denominationalism* (Meridian, New York, 1957)

Radford, L. A., *Ancient Heresies in Modern Dress* (Robertson, Melbourne, 1913)

Ross, K. N., *Dangerous Delusions* (Mowbrays, London, 1961)

Roy, Ralph Lord, *Apostles of Discord* (Beacon Press, Boston, 1953)

Sanders, J. O., & Wright, J. S., *Some Modern Religions* (Tyndale Press, London, 1956, etc.)

Sundkler, Bengt, *Bantu Prophets in South Africa* (Lutterworth Press, London, 1948)

Van Baalen, J. K., *The Chaos of Cults* (Eerdmans, Grand Rapids, Michigan, 1938, etc.)

Wilson, B. R., *Sects and Society: The Sociology of Three Religious Groups in Britain* (Elim Four Square Gospel Church, Christian Science, Christadelphians) (Heinemann, London, 1961)

2

PENTECOSTALISM

*Now, brethren, if I come to you speaking in tongues,
how shall I benefit you unless I bring you some revelation or knowledge or prophecy or teaching?*

(I Cor. 14.6)

PENTECOSTALISM is a movement that attempts to recap-
ture the ardour of primitive Christianity, believing that the
chosen people in the historic Christian Churches have become
the frozen people of God. It is a very comprehensive term
which is applied to a large number of revivalistic sects in the
English-speaking world and beyond, which are primarily concerned with perfection, holiness and the renewal of the Pentecostal experience. The largest of the groups, in itself an alliance
of formerly independent Pentecostal congregations, is the
Assemblies of God. Others among the more important groups
of the wider Pentecostalist movement are the Apostolic Church,
the Elim Foursquare Gospel Alliance, the Church of God,
the Church of God in Christ and the Pentecostal Holiness
Church.

I

It is important at the outset to make clear that Pentecostalism is not a heretical group within Protestantism. They are, in
fact, members of the Evangelical Alliance. All Pentecostalists
are conservative Protestants affirming the doctrines of the Holy
Trinity, original sin, justification by faith, the Deity of Christ,
salvation through the atoning blood of Christ, the Virgin
Birth, the imminent Second Coming of Christ, the bodily
Resurrection and the literal inerrancy of the Holy Scriptures.

The Pentecostalists do not add to revelation like the Mormons, nor do they radically reinterpret the Christian revelation like the Christian Scientists. They appear in this volume as the happy example of increasingly penitent sectarians. That is, they established movements in protest against the paralysing chill that had overtaken much of orthodox Christianity, but now wish to bring that warmth of witness and vigour into the comity of the World Council of Churches.

The challenge of the Pentecostalists is all the more serious because of their rapid recent growth in the English-speaking parts of the world, in Latin-America and in Africa, Dr Henry Pitney Van Dusen, formerly President of Union Theological Seminary in New York City, has called them 'The Third Force' within Christendom. Thereby he suggests that in influence and extent they may well come to rival both Catholicism (Roman and Eastern) and Protestantism if their astronomical rate of growth is maintained. That this is no exaggerated judgment can be shown by considering only the comparative statistics[1] of the combined growth of the Assemblies of God and the Church of God in the United States.

If we limit ourselves only to those bodies which include the term 'Pentecostal' in their titles in the U.S.A. (ignoring the Assemblies of God and the Church of God in the United States, and associated Holiness Groups), we shall discover in the *Yearbook of the American Churches for 1964* that they have a total membership of 292,225. The three largest groups, within this category, are the United Pentecostal Church, Inc., with 150,000 members; the Pentecostal Holiness Church, Inc., with 57,366 members; and Pentecostal Assemblies of the World, Inc., with 45,000 members.

Optimism as to the future needs to be qualified in part, however, by recalling that the Pentecostalists are a twentieth-century mushrooming phenomenon and that there are already signs that in the diminution of emphasis on charismatic phenomena they are making the transition from the sect to the denomination. Ardour almost always cools with the arrival of order. Then, again, the general level of education is rising and

[1] Cf. I. Winehouse, *The Assemblies of God* (1959), pp. 54-5, where it is shown that 50,386 members in 1925 increased to 482,352 in 1958.

this makes it more difficult to maintain rigidly conservative views of the authority of the Bible. Finally, in a world in which the formerly dispossessed coloured peoples are becoming members of independent States (in Africa) or joining the vast middle class (in the United States) a largely segregationist group like the Pentecostalists is not likely to maintain its present impetus. Even after allowing for these factors, however, the rise and spread of Pentecostalism is a truly impressive phenomenon. It is a particularly vigorous and thriving fellowship in South America.

II

The history of Pentecostalism is an important clue to the religious and social needs that it met and to the perpetual necessity in Christ's Church for the renewal of vitality and warmth.

It is, of course, no innovation in the long centuries of Christian history. Remote parallels to it may be found in Montanism (the ecstatic movement fathered by Montanus, the Phrygian ex-priest of Cybele and visionary), as in the spiritual intoxication of the Anabaptists of Zwickau, and in the double emphasis on the Second Advent and the speaking with tongues stressed by Edward Irving, founder of the Catholic Apostolic Church in London in the eighteen-thirties.

Pentecostalism's proximate origins, however, can be traced to three significant nineteenth-century movements which were its tap-roots.[1] This century witnessed the rise of aggressive and conservative evangelical trends in religion in revulsion from the accommodating theological liberalism of the period, which appeared to make religion relevant only at the cost of diluting it. These trends may be given bodies and names by their association with Peter Cartwright, Charles Finney and Dwight L. Moody. In the second place, there was also the rise of Methodist Holiness Associations which re-emphasized Wesley's concern for 'Scriptural holiness' and Christian perfection. Thirdly, there was an added insistence upon the supremacy of the supernatural in Christian faith by the teaching that Christ the Healer could be the Physician of the bodies as well as the souls of men. This was advocated by A. B. Simpson of the

[1] *Ibid.*, pp. 15-16.

Christian and Missionary Alliance in New York and by John
Alexander Dowie through the Zion Movement in Chicago. All
three tap-roots of Pentecostalism represented a return to
vigorous, charismatic, enthusiastic Christian primitivism on
which the trunk, branches and leaves of Pentecostalism could
be fed.

The Pentecostalists themselves claim that the birthday of the
movement was April 9, 1906, and the birthplace a private home
in Los Angeles, California, where some members of the Asuza
Street Mission were meeting under the leadership of the Rev.
W. J. Seymour, a Coloured minister. They were fasting and
praying for the Baptism of the Holy Ghost when the inner,
Divine empowering was felt and some of them spoke ecstatic-
ally in tongues. Such experiences, widely reported in the news-
papers of the day, attracted thousands to Los Angeles and
similar joyful 'Pentecosts' were held throughout the United
States and Canada, as well as in Norway.

The English Pentecostal 'fire' was a torch brought from Norway to the North of England by the Rev. T. B. Barratt, who
had kindled it in Los Angeles. A former Methodist born in
England, he had successfully taught his people in Norway to
pray for the Pentecostal gifts. He, in turn, had been visited by
the Rev. Alexander A. Boddy, the evangelical rector of All
Saints', Monkwearmouth. Boddy invited Barratt to preach at a
special evening service at his church in September, 1907, after
which several experienced the Baptism of the Holy Spirit. The
experience was repeated in Wales, where Maesteg became an
important early centre for Pentecostalism. Here the famous
Jeffreys family founded the remarkably successful Elim Foursquare Gospel Alliance which conducted many successful
revival meetings in Ireland.

III

What, then, was the greatly valued 'Baptism of the Holy
Spirit'? It was certainly something other than the experience
of conversion. In fact, it was described as a 'second blessing'
for believers. Pentecostalists believe that they have the strongest scriptural warrant for seeking this post-conversion blessing.
While recognizing the deep Dispensational significance of the
original Pentecost or Whitsunday, they also insist that the

endowment of 'tongues of fire', and speaking with tongues and seeing visions, was not confined to that single occasion. They point to the facts that there were subsequent local repetitions of that blessing: in Samaria according to Acts 8; at Caesarea according to Acts 10; and twenty-three years later at Ephesus according to Acts 19. As proof that this is a post-baptismal gift, they also insist that the experience of the Baptism of the Holy Spirit took place much later than the Baptism of the same believers at the hands of Philip.

In the words of a sober leader and historian of the English Pentecostalist movement:

> The particular and distinctive testimony of the Pentecostalist Movement has been that the outward evidences that accompanied the Baptism in the Holy Spirit in primitive Christian experience can be, should be, and are being repeated up to date. It is this special witness that has earned for it among its opponents the *sobriquet* of the 'tongues movement'.[1]

Gee asserts that the Pentecostalists teach 'that speaking with tongues is the scriptural initial evidence of that Baptism in the Holy Spirit'.[2] He concludes, moreover, that all Christians should also expect other supernatural gifts today that were characteristic of the life of the Primitive Church and that these include prophesying, healing and visions, as well as tongues. The authority for this belief is found in I Cor. 12-14.

Leaders of the American Assemblies of God provided a sympathetic reporter recently with some vivid descriptions of the phenomena of 'speaking with tongues'. A Mr Flower described the experience thus:

> It is like a power within a person. It rises up within one and takes control of one's vocal organs. An utterance comes out which does not come through the mind. It is an ecstatic utterance. Speaking in tongues is speaking a distinct language unknown to the speaker; sometimes it has been an unknown tongue.[3]

---

[1] Donald Gee, *The Pentecostal Movement* (Elim Publishing Co., London, 1949), pp. 10ff.
[2] *Op. cit.*, p. 8.
[3] Irwin Winehouse, *The Assemblies of God: A Popular Survey* (Vantage Press; New York, Washington, Hollywood, 1959), p. 88.

At the same frank interview Riggs, the President of the American Assemblies of God, volunteered the following information about a recent experience of speaking in tongues:

> One of the workers here was telling us of an experience she had at our camp meeting while kneeling around the altar. She was talking in tongues, praising the Lord, giving utterance in an ecstasy. Kneeling at her side was a little woman who came to her after the service and commented on what she had been saying. The woman asked, 'Do you know what is my language?' She said, 'No! what is your language?' The woman said she came from a province of Yugoslavia, and that this worker had been speaking her language perfectly, naming people and places that she had known in her home country. The girl had never been out of the United States.[1]

It is only just to Pentecostalists, however, to indicate that not all of them believe that speaking in tongues is uttering a foreign language. Mr Donald Gee, for example, does not scruple to admit that in the early days of the Pentecostal Movement there was a tendency to seek for identification of the languages spoken, 'doubtless because of the traditional, but mistaken and unscriptural, view that the gift of tongues was for preaching the gospel to the heathen'.[2]

All Pentecostalists, then, are distinguished from other ultra-conservative Protestant sects by the primary importance given to the speaking in tongues. Moreover, they would emphasize in the strongest manner that, as the gift of tongues was delivered to the infant Christian community at the beginning of the Christian dispensation, so the present pouring out of the Holy Spirit is a token that Christ's return is imminent. These signs of tongues, visions, prophecies and healings are, therefore, the marks of 'the end of these days'. The important cohesion the acceptance of these convictions gives to Pentecostalists was publicly manifested in the great international gatherings held in recent decades. The Pentecostalists have held impressive world conferences in Stockholm, Zürich, Paris, London, Toronto, Jerusalem, Helsinki, in the last twenty-five years.

Nonetheless, it is important to recognize that it is an Asso-

[1] *Ibid.*, p. 89.   [2] *The Pentecostal Movement*, p. 38.

ciation, not a vast new denomination. In other words, there are differences among the Pentecostalists. The largest of all the groups is known as the Assemblies of God, which is growing in the United States at the rate of a new church planted every day. It has half a million church members in the U.S.A., 922,000 children in Sunday schools, and has established 61 Foreign Bible Schools, while it has nine colleges and Bible institutes in the United States. Its foreign membership is almost three-quarters of a million and its 775 foreign missionaries are serving in 69 different countries.[1] Affiliated with it is the Church of God and it has friendly relationships with the Negro Pentecostalist denomination, the Church of God in Christ, with headquarters in Memphis, Tennessee. It also recognizes its spiritual kinship (though no formal relationship) with the group founded by the sensational and vivacious Aimee Semple McPherson, foundress of the International Church of the Foursquare Gospel, which made more rapid strides after her death than during her final years. For example, most Pentecostalists accept with the utmost readiness the four tenets that make up the Christology of the 'Foursquare Gospel'—that Christ is the Saviour, the Healer, the Baptizer in the Holy Spirit and the Coming King. Finally, the same spiritual kinship is acknowledged as existing between the Assemblies of God and the Pentecostal Holiness Church recently brought to the forefront by the dramatic faith-healing sessions of Oral Roberts which are televised on Sundays on a nation-wide programme in the United States. There are also many other smaller Pentecostalist groups in the United States.

In Britain the Pentecostalists seem to be divided into three groups: the Assemblies of God, the Apostolic Church, and the Elim Foursquare Gospel Alliance (not related to the Aimee Semple McPherson group in the U.S.A.). The Assemblies of God are the largest group and they work in close unity with the Elim Church. The relations of these two groups with the Apostolic Church were once suspicious but are now harmonious. All are now equal members of the British Pentecostal Fellowship. Differences of emphasis remain.

In the first place, the Assemblies of God give autonomy to the local churches which are loosely federated into the larger

[1] Statistics from Irwin Winehouse, *op. cit.*, pp. 197-8.

denominational association. At the outset there were several local groups under the natural leadership of devout men and they valued their independency which they intended to maintain. The Elim Foursquare Gospel Alliance, however, has retained a separate identity because it organized great revivalistic mass meetings with great success under the ruggedly eloquent leadership of the Jeffreys family of Maesteg in South Wales and the converts in both Wales and Ireland felt a sense of indebtedness and loyalty to this particular organization which they desired to retain. This, however, does not prevent them from close co-operation with the Assemblies of God.

The Apostolic Church, on the other hand, is a denomination with strong control from the centre which was criticized by the other two Pentecostalist denominations because it gained many proselytes from Elim and the Assemblies before they organized themselves into denominations in self-defence.[1] The Apostolics claimed to have received more vision than the other Pentecostal groups and in the light of this were recovering not only the supernatural endowments of the Primitive Church, but also the early Apostolic forms of church order and government. For the Apostolic Church this had to have the five-fold structure of apostles, prophets, pastors, elders and deacons. The self-styled 'apostles' claimed an absolute authority which was regarded as tyranny by the loosely organized congregations that united to become the Assemblies of God. Moreover, it was also felt that the 'prophets' of the Apostolic Church were erratic, extravagant and inconsistent in their visionary claims. In short, the presence of an absolute hierarchy in the Apostolic Church was strongly at variance with the democratic organization and the general expression of the priesthood of all believers that marked the fellowship of the majority of the Pentecostal local communities.

IV

If speaking in tongues and the practice of faith-healing are distinctive characteristics of all groups in the Pentecostal Movement, this is far from exhausting the nature of the Christian life as they conceive it. It is natural, therefore, to consider

[1] See the criticisms of Donald Gee in *The Pentecostal Movement*, pp. 106-7.

their worship, the distinctive quality of their ministries, and their ethical standards.

A strongly non-liturgical group, theirs is a free worship with extemporary prayers, believed to be prompted by the Holy Spirit. They assert that forms breed formalism, yet their own type of worship with its 'sandwich' form (in which the bread is represented by the hymns and the prayers, lessons and sermon are the 'meat') is fairly stereotyped. Even so, the place given to speaking in tongues always allows for the impact of the unpredictable Holy Spirit. They celebrate the Sacraments of Believers' Baptism and the Lord's Supper.

Since the Pentecostalists are often the church of the underprivileged, they not only value gospel hymns with refrains, the punctuation of prayers with 'Hallelujahs' and first-hand, rather emotional, testimonies, but they have also been remarkably successful in certain specialized ministries to the social outcasts in which the older Churches would do well to emulate their spirit and example. For instance, they have an important ministry to prisoners and have even set up correspondence courses in the Bible for convicts who find a genuine welcome in the Pentecostal fellowships on their return to the world that outlawed them. The Assemblies of God in the U.S.A. have a splendidly effective ministry to minority ethnic groups also. Their foreign-language branch churches include preaching and worship in the German, Greek, Hungarian, Italian, Polish, Russian and Spanish languages. They have 561 such congregations ministering to 38,000 members.[1] In Assuat in Egypt they maintain an orphanage with 1,200 children and in West Africa a leprosarium and a town of rehabilitated lepers which is deservedly called New Hope. They also have a popular and relevant radio ministry on many stations in the United States. In all these ways their initiative and zeal are wholly admirable.

Perhaps the best brief description of the nature of Pentecostalism has been offered by one of their Norwegian members in the following words:

On the question of Justification by Faith they are Lutherans, on Baptism Baptists, on Sanctification early Methodists, in their work of winning souls Salvationists; but with

---

[1] Irwin Winehouse, *op. cit.*, p. 145.

regard to Baptism with the Holy Spirit they are Pentecostalists, as they believe and preach that it is possible to be baptized in or filled by the Holy Spirit as on the day of Pentecost.[1]

The only addition that needs to be made is that on matters of church government most of them are Congregationalists.

Ethically, they are world-condemning pietists for whom the Bible is a rigid code of laws applicable to all conditions and all circumstances of life. Their views may briefly be gathered from the statement made by President Riggs, the leader of the Assemblies of God in the United States: 'We have membership cards on which a person who has joined the Church declares he will not use liquor, or tobacco, or engage in dancing.'[2] The use of cosmetics, while not prohibited, is definitely disliked. What is perhaps more disturbing than this negativism in ethics is that Pentecostalists do not appear to be interested in such problems of Christian social ethics as social justice or the removal of the colour-bar. Their negative and world-renouncing ethic can easily become a refined form of primary concern for their own salvation in the hereafter and the neglect of the reign of God in present society which they have already written off as 'enemy-occupied territory'. But, in fact, they have proved more successful in effecting conversions than any Protestant denomination. They have an approximate world community of ten millions.

V

An attempt at a just evaluation of the doctrine and practices of the Pentecostalists would require us again to insist that they are orthodox biblically conservative Protestant Christians, and not heretics. Their intense and fervid faith, the warmth and generosity of their fellowships, their missionary zeal and support of their charitable institutions, as well as their specialized ministries to prisoners and lepers, are wholly admirable and authentically Christian. Moreover, many second-generation Pentecostalists have become excellent members of the historic Christian Churches, adding to their unabated zeal a concern for

[1] Einar Molland, *Christendom* (Mowbrays, London, and Philosophical Library, New York, 1959), p. 303.
[2] Irwin Winehouse, *op. cit.*, p. 85.

the relationship of Christianity to culture and for the Gospel's transformation of the socio-economic life of the world. This, in itself, is an indication of the narrowness of first-generation Pentecostalism, with its ethics of flight rather than fight, and its uncharitable insistence that the Churches have utterly betrayed Christ. This 'holier-than-thou' attitude reflects pride rather than Christian humility and is the very parent vine that produces the sour grapes of sectarianism.

The charismatic phenomena, which they believe to be the proof of the enduring Pentecostal experience, caused St Paul considerable anxiety in the Corinthian Church, as they may well for twentieth-century Christians. The problem is how to distinguish between edifying and unedifying experiences.[1] The Assemblies of God, for example, are critical of the place given to 'prophecy' by the Apostolic Church, yet prophecies and visions are as truly characteristic of the experience of the first-century Church as faith-healing and speaking in tongues. Moreover, while the Pentecostalists point to Mark 16.17-18 as their charter from the Gospel itself for speaking in tongues, they have no satisfactory explanation for the omission of the other signs of the supernatural Spirit's being in their midst. The declaration which begins, 'In my name they shall cast out demons; they shall speak with new tongues' continues with the words: 'they shall take up serpents; and if they drink any deadly thing, it shall in no wise hurt them.' Yet Pentecostalists neither drink poison nor coil cobras about their necks to demonstrate the perfection of the Divine protection.

St Paul's criterion is that the enduringly significant Christian experiences must 'edify', that is, build up men and women in the faith, rather than be confusing or sensational manifestations of the Holy Spirit. It is surely important that in I Cor. 13 faith, hope and love are declared to abide, but that tongues shall cease. Furthermore, when St Paul lists the fruits of the Spirit in Gal. 5.22-25 tongues are entirely excluded. We may draw the conclusion, therefore, that the Pentecostalists are attempting to preserve as an enduring manifestation of the Holy Spirit what was intended to be only a temporary and ephemeral disclosure of power.

[1] See H. J. Stolee, *Pentecostalism; the Problem of the Modern Tongues Movement* (Minneapolis, Minnesota, 1936).

Any positive response to the Pentecostal Movement on the part of the historic Christian Churches must recognize that they have important lessons to teach. The first is that formalism can be even more deadly to the Christian life than fanaticism. The second is that, to quote Dr Emil Brunner, 'the Church exists for mission as the fire does for burning'. The Pentecostalists are willing to stand up and be counted; they never creep into the shadows like those who are uncertain of their allegiance. The historic Churches must teach their members to live with conviction and compassion, nourished by a living faith in the God whose promises are always kept. The success of the 'Third Force' in Christendom should summon the First and Second Forces to more strenuous warfare in the unending combat between God and the modern forms of idolatry.

Further reading

du Plessis, David J., *The Spirit Bade Me Go* (author-publisher, 3472 Linwood Ave., Oakland, California, 1963)

Gee, Donald, *The Pentecostal Movement* (Elim Publishing Co., London, 1949)

Molland, Einar, *Christendom* (Mowbrays, London, and Philosophical Library, New York, 1959), chap. XV.

Stolee, H. J., *Pentecostalism: The Problem of the Modern Tongues Movement* (Ausgburg Publishing House, Minneapolis, Minnesota, 1936)

Webster, Douglas, *Pentecostalism and Speaking with Tongues* (Highway Press, London, 1965)

Winehouse, Irwin, *The Assemblies of God: A Popular Survey* (Vantage Press, New York, Washington, Hollywood, 1959)

3

SEVENTH-DAY ADVENTISM

*Now therefore why tempt ye God, that ye should put
a yoke upon the neck of the disciples, which neither
our fathers nor we were able to bear?*

(Acts 15.10)

THIS millenarian movement, which has flourished among underprivileged peoples and classes, claims that it is the only true Church because it alone keeps the fourth Commandment inviolate by observing the Sabbath on the seventh day, whereas the rest of Christendom observes it on the first day of the week. Its followers, the Seventh-Day Adventists declare, alone will be among the 144,000 elect who will attain to everlasting life.

How then, does such an odd creed commend itself to hundreds of thousands of adherents? In the first place, it has an army of aggressive evangelists; it does not, like so many Churches, leave witnessing to the professionals. These evangelists would shame most Christians by their thorough, if literal, acquaintance with the Bible, which they are able to quote volubly, with references to chapter and verse. Even their Adventism, despite the crudity of some of its teaching, represents a two-fold protest against both the modernism that teaches an inevitable progress towards Utopia and the less refined traditionalism that clings to a belief in a Hell where the damned suffer everlasting torments. In opposition to both of these concepts, Seventh-Day Adventism declares that the Second Advent will take place quietly (no blood-curdling Armageddon will bring the new world order in) and that evil-doers will be annihilated, not subjected to eternal tortures.

These factors account, at least partially, for the numerical success of this sect which originated, like so many others, in the United States of America in the nineteenth century. In the U.S.A. the Seventh-Day Adventists have a membership of 335,765, as reported in the *Yearbook of the American Churches for 1964*.

I

The movement cannot be understood apart from a brief account of its history. As in the case of Christian Science and Theosophy, Seventh-Day Adventism had a female founder, Ellen Harmon, though she is better known under her married name, as Mrs Ellen White. She shares with Mrs Mary Baker Eddy another peculiarity—she did not admit her theological loans! Just as Mrs Eddy leaned heavily upon the teaching of the quack Quimby, without acknowledging her indebtedness, so did Mrs White pick the brains of William Miller, the founder of the Adventists.

William Miller was a Baptist, born at Pittsfield, Massachusetts, in 1782, who was educated at Low Hampton in New York State. This farmer studied the Bible with extraordinary zeal, but without historical knowledge or critical acumen, and announced in 1831 that he had discovered the exact date of Christ's Second Coming. He declared confidently that, on the basis of the predictions of Daniel and Revelation, this event would take place in 1843. When nothing happened during this year, he admitted a mistake in his calculations and postponed the fulfilment of his prophecy to the following year. When he was again proved wrong, he gave up Adventism. In his significant renunciation, he stated:

> On the passing of the published time, I frankly acknowledged my disappointment. We expected the personal coming of Christ at that time; and now to contend that we were not mistaken is dishonest. We should never be ashamed frankly to confess our errors. I have no confidence in any of the new theories that grew out of that movement, namely, that Christ then came as the Bridegroom, that the door of mercy was closed, that there is no salvation for sinners, that the seventh trumpet then sounded, or that it was a fulfilment of prophecy in any sense.[1]

[1] *History of the Advent Message*, pp. 410, 412.

Despite his recantation, Ellen Harmon (White), an intense young woman, persisted in believing that his prophecies were substantially correct, and founded a sect, named the Seventh-Day Adventists. They held the view that

> the Lord did really come in 1844, not to the earth, but to cleanse the sanctuary in Heaven . . . The Lord passed into the sanctuary in 1844, which Mrs White was taken up to Heaven and shown.[1]

They believed that our Lord then cleansed the sanctuary and commenced the Final Judgment, closing the door of mercy to sinners. They claimed that only those who knew about the 'change' could benefit by his mediation. Others, according to Ellen White, 'offer up their useless prayers to the apartment which Jesus left'.[2] Salvation was made to depend on knowledge of an event in 1844 of which only the Seventh-Day Adventists had heard, and upon the observance of the Jewish Sabbath in place of the Christian Lord's Day. The latter tradition of Christendom is named 'The Mark of the Beast' by Seventh-Day Adventists. Their greatest claim is that they are alone in preaching the three messages referred to in Rev. 14.6-12, that 'the seal of God is the holy Sabbath' and that the 144,000 of Rev. 7.1-8, who are to be translated at the Advent, are now being sealed.

II

The unique beliefs of the Seventh-Day Adventists must now be considered in detail. The first feature is, of course, their teaching on Adventism. Now, although the founder of the Adventist movement, William Miller, admitted that his predictions had been erroneous, Mrs White refused to give up the idea of a predicted Advent. Mr D. M. Canright, a former elder of the sect, informs us in his *Seventh-Day Adventism Renounced* that he was taught that 'the Judgment of the World had started already in 1844, and that the End of the World was to be expected in this generation'.

The assertion that Christ entered into the sanctuary of Heaven to effect its cleansing was the doctrine discovered by Mrs White which gave a significance to the year 1844. This,

[1] *Early Writings*, pp. 114-15.   [2] *Spiritual Gifts*, p. 172.

however, was done only at the cost of a severe distortion of the New Testament teaching on the Atonement. She held that the work of our Lord was not finished on earth in the days of his Passion, because 'as the closing portion of his work as priest, before he takes his throne as King, he will make the great atonement'.[1] According to her, Christ entered only the outer sanctuary at the Ascension, not the holy of holies, although this is clearly contradicted by Heb. 1.3.

The third and most prominent element in their teaching is the insistence upon a seventh-day Sabbath. This position they defend on biblical and historical grounds. While Mrs Ellen White admitted that the New Covenant had done away with the Old Covenant of Moses, she yet held that the moral, as distinct from the ceremonial precepts of the Law were still binding on Christians. She went on to argue that since the observance of the Sabbath on the seventh day occurs as one of the commandments of the moral law, therefore the observance of the Sabbath on the seventh day is unrepealed and is a perpetual obligation on Christians. To substantiate this teaching, Mrs White claimed to have had a vision of the sanctuary in Heaven where

> Jesus raised the cover of the ark, and she beheld the tables of stone on which the ten commandments were written. She was amazed as she saw the Fourth Commandment in the very centre of the ten precepts, with a soft halo of light encircling it.[2]

The historical claim of the Seventh-Day Adventists that the Churches fell into apostasy in this matter rests on the assertion that the Council of Laodicea in AD 364 changed the Sabbath or seventh day to Sunday or the first day of the week.

They further teach that Jesus Christ inherited a fallen human nature, as may be gathered from the following citation:

> In his humanity Christ partook of our sinful, fallen nature. If not, then he was not 'made like unto us his brethren', was not 'in all points tempted like as we are', did

[1] *Fundamental Principles.*
[2] Cited W. C. Irvine, *Heresies Exposed* (Pickering and Inglis, 8th edn., 1937), p. 149.

not overcome as we have to overcome, and is not therefore the complete and perfect Saviour man needs and must have to be saved.[1]

Their final distinctive doctrine is their belief in the sleep of the soul after death. The state of the dead is said to be 'one of silence, inactivity and entire unconsciousness'. The five proof texts for this doctrine, all significantly taken from the Old Testament, are: Psalm 146.4; Eccles. 9.5, 6, 10; Dan. 12.2.

III

Seventh-Day Adventist beliefs must be considered with care. This is warranted both by their rapid spread through many parts of the world and by the closeness of much of their teaching to historic Christianity.

This group lacks the charity which should characterize the company of those to whom Christ addressed the words, 'I have called you friends, not servants'. None the less, the Seventh-Day Adventists acknowledge themselves alone to be among the 144,000 elect and castigate all the Churches which celebrate the Lord's Day on the first day of the week (the rest of Christendom, no less) as 'Babylon', bearing 'the mark of the Beast'.

Their insistence upon the necessity for keeping the seventh day or Jewish Sabbath as one of the main articles of faith on which salvation depends is both foreign to the New Testament in its declension from grace to legalism and deficient in any true sense of Christian proportion. Furthermore, its assertion that the change from the seventh day Sabbath to the first day Sunday was made by the Council of Laodicea is unhistorical.

Col. 2.14 rightly reminds us that 'the hand-writing of ordinances' (the Law of Moses) was 'blotted out' and nailed to Christ's Cross, as in ancient times old bills were nailed to the doorpost when paid. Since Christ has met every claim of the Law on our behalf, its precepts are no longer obligatory on Christians. The distinction which Mrs White made between ceremonial and moral law is entirely unknown in the Old Testament, as a perusal of Ex. 24.3 will show conclusively. Furthermore, it is difficult to understand how she could have

[1] *Bible Readings for the Home Circle* (1915 edn.), p. 115.

regarded the matter of observing a particular day as more holy than another as a moral issue, when it is more obviously a matter of ceremonial import. In any case, Christians believe in the supremacy of grace over law, whereas she would make the New Testament a new Leviticus. The New Testament shows us that even the moral law of the Old Testament is superseded. The Old Testament declares 'Thou shalt not kill'. But this negative precept is replaced in the New Testament by the more positive and penetrating counsel, 'If thine enemy hunger, feed him; if he thirst, give him drink'.

The grace of our Lord Jesus Christ frees us from empty ceremonial and scrupulous adherence to the letter of the Law. St Augustine insisted that all the ethical precepts of Christianity could be summed up in the injunction: 'Love God and do what you like.' In short, this doctrine of the Seventh-Day Adventists is an irrelevant legalism in the life of the Spirit. It is already condemned in the words of Col. 2.16-17, 'Let no man therefore judge you in meat, or in drink, or in respect of an holy day, or of the new moon, or of the sabbath days, which are a shadow of things to come; but the body is of Christ.'

There is, moreover, a positive reason for the change from the seventh day to the first for the celebration of the Lord's Day during the Christian dispensation. The old Sabbath was a memorial of the origin of life; the new Sabbath, commemorating Christ's resurrection, is a memorial of the victory of life over death. In the felicitous words of Dr Lewis Radford:

> The old Sabbath marked the close of the first stage of divine activity, Creation; the new Lord's Day marks the beginning of the second stage, Regeneration. The Sabbath ended the week with a *Nunc Dimittis* of resignation; the Lord's Day begins the week with a *Te Deum* of renewal.[1]

Even the claim that the Council of Laodicea introduced the change from the celebration of the Jewish Sabbath to the Christian Lord's Day is unwarranted. In the first place, this was an Eastern Council and was therefore not authoritative for the more important Western Churches. In the second place, it merely forbade Christians from abstaining from work on the

[1] L. B. Radford, *Ancient Heresies in Modern Dress* (Robertson, Melbourne, 1913), p. 78.

Jewish Sabbath, calling this practice 'Judaizing'. In fact, there is evidence to show that the Lord's Day was generally celebrated on the first day of the week in the second century. *The Epistle to Barnabas* (early second century) records: 'Wherefore, also, we keep the eighth day with joyfulness, the day also on which Jesus rose from the dead.' And Justin Martyr, writing about the middle of the second century, declares: 'But Sunday is the day on which we all hold a common assembly, because it is the first day of the week on which God . . . made the world; and Jesus Christ our Saviour on the same day rose from the dead.'

The most overwhelming indictment of the sabbatarianism of this group is offered by Dr James Black:

> To found a church on that ancient, outlived and outdated Jewish Sabbath passes comprehension. There are so many big things worth fighting for. Why fight for a shadow?[1]

Our third criticism must be of the Adventism of the group. Their system is weakened by a misconception of the function of prophecy. They assume that the prophets's task is to foretell the course of events like an inspired crystal-gazer. Beyond the immediate horizon of the prophet there is only the vision of the final victory of the Kingdom of God. The prophet tells of the consequence of unrighteousness and predicts the joy of the people of God if they repent, but he does not predict events in detail. If he did, this would make his offer of salvation to be freely accepted meaningless, for a predetermined future and an appeal to change the heart are incompatible. In any case, the Seventh-Day Adventists go beyond the statement of our Lord in their claims for He declared of the Second Advent, 'No man knoweth the hour, . . . not even the Son'. Seventh-Day Adventists presumably lay claim to a higher revelation than that vouchsafed to the Messiah.

Fourthly, the Seventh-Day Adventists in their doctrine of the sanctuary would destroy the true significance of the Ascension of our Lord and of His Priesthood. They claim that there were two stages in our Lord's High Priesthood, corresponding to the Jewish high priest's ministrations first in the outer chamber and

[1] *New Forms of the Old Faith*, p. 221.

then in the inner chamber of the earthly tabernacle. But the Epistle to the Hebrews (9.24) represents Jesus as entering into the inmost sanctuary of the presence of God, not merely to purify the heavenly things, but 'now to appear before the face of God for us'. In the New Testament purifying and appearing are clearly two aspects of the one fact. Adventists have, therefore, no shred of biblical evidence for their fantastic belief that the appearance of the perfect Man to present his sacrifice of obedience even unto death took place in AD 1844. The writer of Hebrews (8.1) believed that it took place at the Ascension.

Dr Radford draws out the logical consequences of this belief, with its denial of the New Testament doctrine that Christ 'ever liveth to make intercession for us', in the comment:

> Adventism stands committed to the amazing theory that for eighteen centuries the ascended Christ was still waiting to enter the sanctuary of the presence of God and to prepare the heavenly world for the approach of man to God . . . If this atoning entry took place in 1844, what was the scene, the character, the efficacy of His activity for those eighteen centuries of human time?[1]

The effect of this belief is also to reduce the function of the Holy Spirit during eighteen centuries to being the minister of the unfinished work of the Father and the Son.

The assertion that the intermediate state after death is one of entire unconsciousness can find Old Testament warrants, but is entirely contradicted by the New Testament. The latter teaches or implies that the soul is conscious in the unseen world. The parable of Lazarus (Luke 16.22-25), the promise our Lord made to the dying thief (Luke 23.43), the impatient cry of the waiting martyrs (Rev. 6.9-11), the wish of St Paul (Phil. 1.21), and the missionary activity of the human spirit of the Christ among the departed between His death and His resurrection (I Pet. 3.19 and 4.6) controvert the assertions of the Seventh-Day Adventists.

Finally, their erroneous interpretations in the past awaken suspicion and leave little room for confidence in their distinctive doctrines. On two occasions their predictions of the Second Advent have been proved false. They once began their Sabbath

[1] *Ancient Heresies in Modern Dress*, p. 87.

at six in the evening, but changed the time when they discovered that the biblical Sabbath began at sunset. There was a time when they enforced a vegetarian diet on their adherents; once they condemned all religious organization and political voting as 'marks of the Beast'; once they prevented their children from attending and being contaminated by State schools. None of these practices is now insisted upon. Their official explanation that the Lord was trying their faith by disappointments was convenient, but it is not wholly convincing.

On the whole, then, their claims suggest that their distinctive doctrines are partly the products of computation and speculation. They have no New Testament warrant. These considerations must make for difficulty in any approaches made to the Adventists by the historic Churches. Even so, the approach must be made.

Further reading

Froom, L. R. E., *The Prophetic Faith of Our Fathers* (4 vols., Washington, 1946-54)

Olsen, M. E., *A History of the Origin and Progress of the Seventh Day Adventists* (Tacoma Park, 2nd ed., 1926)

Spalding, A. W., *Captains of the Host* (1949) and *Christ's Last Legion* (1949). Both published by the *Review and Herald*, Washington, D.C., the former a history up to 1900 and the latter a history since 1900

Critiques:

Bird, Herbert S., *Theology of Seventh-Day Adventism* (Grand Rapids: Eerdmans, 1961)

Mitchell, David, *Seventh-Day Adventists: Faith in Action* (New York: Vantage Press, 1958—a very sympathetic account by a non-Adventist)

4

MORAL RE-ARMAMENT

*We reckon therefore that a man is justified by faith
apart from the works of the law.*

(Rom. 3.28)

Is the former Oxford Group Movement, now styled Moral
Re-Armament, a foe or friend of the historic Christian
Churches? This question has been asked and answered with a
new vigour and thoroughness in a 'battle of the books' in 1964.
The protagonists are both members of the Church of England,
but they come to a very different judgment. Mr Tom Driberg,
a Labour Member of Parliament, in *The Mystery of Moral
Re-Armament*, while admitting that the movement has stressed
'teachings about the reality of guidance and the necessity of
repentance in fellowship', concludes that M.R.A. is 'essentially
non-Christian and anti-democratic'.[1] The Rev. J. P. Thornton-
Duesbery, Master of St Peter's College, Oxford, in *The Open
Secret of M.R.A.* believes that the core of the leadership of the
movement consists of 'dedicated Christian men and women'
who are what 'they have aspired to be—commando forces of
the Church, pioneering where the larger body cannot always
go, bringing back many alive to their allegiance to Christ and
enlarging the name and claim of God in the world'.[2]

I

As in the case of many new impulses of the religious or moral
spirit, the Movement cannot be understood apart from some

[1] P. 305.
[2] P. 7. Note the transition from a military to a 'big-game hunt-
ing' metaphor!

knowledge of the odyssey of its founder, the Lutheran minister, the Rev. Dr Frank Buchman (1878-1961).

He was born of German-Swiss stock in the small town of Pennsburg, Pennsylvania, and educated at the co-educational high school, Perkiomen Seminary, which had been founded by the Schwenkfelders, a pietistical group with a strong belief in the direct illumination by God of the human soul. This, so Driberg asserts with considerable probability, may be the origin of Buchman's conviction of the reality of Divine guidance.[1] He received the usual training for the Lutheran ministry. It was begun at Muhlenberg College in Allentown and completed at Mount Airy Theological Seminary on the outskirts of Philadelphia. His first charge was the impoverished Lutheran congregation in Overbrook in his native State, whither he had deliberately gone because a college friend had accused him of overweening personal ambition. Here he founded a boys' settlement and later resigned his charge after a disagreement with the trustees. He then became a dynamic Y.M.C.A. secretary at Pennsylvania State University.

A distinguished Lutheran church historian, Dr Theodore Tappert, believes that the formative influences on Dr Buchman, and, therefore on the future Oxford Group, are 'a combination of pietism and the Y.M.C.A. movement' and that 'the emphasis on a sharp conversion experience' was typical of the Lutheran pietism of the eighteenth century which he inherited. If to this we add the Schwenkfeldian emphasis on Divine and direct guidance, and American advertising technique, as well as the evangelical reinforcement which Buchman received while at a Keswick convention in England, these would seem to be the essential components of the earlier phase of the Oxford Group Movement. It would not, perhaps, be unfair to describe Dr Buchman as a vigorous exponent of dynamic moralistic pietism. Such a phrase is not intended in any pejorative sense, but as a term which defines the intense personal devotion to Christ, the insistence upon rigorous moral standards, and the conviction that the real church consists of warmed hearts committed to witness—the *ecclesiola* or 'little church' within the Church.

Because he had found peace of mind by submitting his own

[1] *Op. cit.*, pp. 21-2.

will to the will of God, he was convinced that religion was not essentially a matter of the intellect, nor even of the heart, but of the will. His life's work would be dedicated to persuading others to live by the will of God, through sharing his own experience. The element of the confession of sins and victory over them became paramount in his thinking at this time. With his characteristic gift for terse and telegrammatic utterance, he summed it up as follows: 'the degree of our freedom from sin is the degree of our desire to be free'. The pietism was expressed in two age-old but newly rediscovered techniques: 'Sharing' and 'Guidance' with the purpose of 'Life-Changing'. 'Sharing' was, in fact, the confession of sins, either privately or before a small group, which marked the reality of repentance and the new beginning of the Christian life. It also took the positive form of mutual encouragement in the victory over past failures. The moralism was mixed with the pietism in the technique of 'Guidance'. It was believed that the new life in Christ must be marked by the 'Four Absolutes': Absolute Honesty, Absolute Purity, Absolute Unselfishness, and Absolute Love, and that for those gathered for their 'Quiet Time' God would provide detailed directions for the duties of each day. The religious discipline for attaining these rigoristic four absolutes was described as follows:

1. The Sharing of our sins and temptations with another Christian life given to God, and to use Sharing as witness to help others, still unchanged, to recognize and acknowledge their sins.
2. Surrender of our life, past, present, and future, into God's keeping and direction.
3. Restitution to all whom we have wronged directly or indirectly.
4. Listening to, accepting, relying on God's Guidance and carrying it out in everything we do or say, great or small.[1]

In the disenchantment of the post-war years in England, as in the ironically-named 'Gilded Age' of the United States, there was a vacuum of the soul which Buchman proceeded to fill with Christian convictions and moral standards. His meetings

[1] The Layman with a Notebook, *What is the Oxford Group?* (Oxford University Press, 1933), p. 7.

were characterized by the brilliant informality of 'house-parties', so that the movement became what has been called 'the Salvation Army of the middle classes'.

The first house-party was held in Kuling in China, in 1918, at the home of a prominent lawyer, and was attended by over a hundred guests.

In 1921 there was organized *A First Century Christian Fellowship*, under which name the movement was first known. The name *Oxford Group* was first used in South Africa by newspapermen in 1929 and from 1934 onwards it was regularly employed. The change to *Moral Re-Armament* which may have been presaged in a speech of Buchman's at East Ham Town Hall on 29 May 1938, came to the forefront in the second World War and after. This represented at least a partial change of outlook and activity. While 'God-control' and 'life-changing' were still stressed, the main thrust of the propaganda of the movement was now on providing an ideology to equip democracy for its struggle against materialism in general, and dialectical materialism (Communism) in particular. Although this diminution of emphasis on the specifically *Christian* and evangelical character of the earlier movement is officially denied, yet it is difficult to see how an ideology for democracy which is commended to Shintoists and Buddhists in Japan, and to Hindus and Buddhists in India and Ceylon, can be anything but vaguely theistic, far less Christocentric. It is precisely this later preference for an ideology for democracy, in lieu of the older and simpler Christian revivalism with some social sophistication, which raises the greatest question as to the *Christian* nature of Moral Re-Armament today.

The chief centres of Moral Re-Armament are to be found in a complex of hotels in Caux, Switzerland, in the impressive Mackinac Island off the shores of Lake Michigan in the U.S.A., and in Odowara in Japan, the newest. One of the most interesting developments is the use of the Westminster Theatre in London for the putting-on of M.R.A. plays which have often gone on tour in various parts of the world. Amongst the most widely seen of such propaganda plays are *The Forgotten Factor, The Good Road,* and *The Vanishing Island* chiefly the work of the imaginative journalist, Peter Howard. Here again there is an ingenious revival of an old Christian technique, developed in the medieval morality and miracle plays and resuscitated in the distinguished Canterbury plays written for and promoted by the Church of England and of which three eminent examples were T. S. Eliot's *Murder in the Cathedral*, Dorothy L. Sayers's *The Zeal of Thy House* and Christopher Fry's *The Lady's Not for Burning* and *The Sleep of Prisoners*.

Of the ingenuity of the M.R.A. there is no question, nor of its capacity to attract many lapsed or nominal Christians as well as non-Christians. The real question is whether its present core of Christian leaders are committed to the historic and incarnation-centred faith (or some increasingly diluted and moralistic version of it) and whether they are commando forces of the Church or diversionary ideological deviationists.[1]

II

Moral Re-Armament has undoubtedly many advantages that commend it to the modern world, and it has developed or revived techniques for commending its views, some of which might well be imitated by the historic Churches today.

There must be appreciation, deep appreciation, for any movement which in the present era of ethical relativity makes a valiant stand for the moral values of our Judaeo-Christian civilization in the West and for spiritual brotherhood in the East. If M.R.A. were still more obviously tied to its pietistical Christian origins than appears to be the case in its recent ideological phase, much more could be said on its behalf. For example, its stress on the conversion of the individual as proven in the 'changed' life with its concomitant demand for restitution to those wronged, for the witness of 'sharing', and for the devotion of time and money in the cause, were all admirable.

It has (or had) a gift for terse and relevant 'translation' of the terms of the Christian faith and life into modern speech. The

[1] While one may accept the claim of the Rev. J. P. Thornton-Duesbery that the veterans of the M.R.A. from Oxford Group days are a Christian core leadership, there is great point in Driberg's question: 'Whether it can still be classified as a Christian movement or sect, it is clear that M.R.A. has become primarily a morale-building and propagandist instrument in the Cold War' (*op. cit.*, p. 150).

attempt to do this has been wholly admirable, even though the achievement has, as is natural, often suffered from slickness or a spurious simplicity. One is not entirely convinced with the assurance that this was 'milk for babes' because there is little evidence that the babes are encouraged to grow up to appreciate the 'strong meat of the Gospel'. But this is surely better than to rely on outworn phrases and *clichés*, as Christian orthodoxy has so often done.

Moral Re-Armament has discovered or rediscovered useful new techniques for commending its convictions. The strategy of house-parties, of public meetings for testimony, and the use of religious drama are three very potent examples of ingenious initiative.

In recent years M.R.A. has paid great attention to the attempt (without radical socio-economic reorganization) to solve industrial and political conflicts across class and racial barriers, with some degree of success. Many well-known labour leaders and parliamentarians, as well as statesmen, have either associated themselves with the Movement or spoken on its platforms. Undoubtedly, one of the greatest reasons for the present interest in the M.R.A. is its public posture as the defender of a moral ideology as an alternative to Communism in the West.

Finally, the newcomer (unless he is an impenitent introvert) is bound to be impressed by the *camaraderie* of the M.R.A., its sense of commitment to the cause, and the disciplined and dedicated lives of its supporters. Cumulatively, these characteristics of the Movement are, at least in part, sufficient to account for its success. They also help to explain the ambiguity of its status by which it is both lauded and criticized by different leaders and members of many branches of the Christian Church.

III

All human movements, however august their claims to Divine origination, inspiration and support, are *mixed* communities. It has hitherto counted severely against the Oxford Group and M.R.A. that however much this has been admitted privately, the public posture was that of an infallible perfectionist organization, inordinately sensitive to criticism. It is, therefore, all the more welcome that the Rev. J. P. Thornton-Duesbery in *The Open Secret of M.R.A.* openly admits the fallibility of the Movement. 'There are,' he writes, 'imperfections in M.R.A. There were in Buchman, as he was himself the first to admit. M.R.A. is no panacea for every human ill, although there *is* a panacea as we shall presently see.' He continues this open-minded admission, with what the present writer can only concede is a sincere but exaggerated claim, that 'my years of observation have steadily strengthened my conviction that, whatever its shortcomings, the Hand of God is upon it and in it, and that to miss the sight of this is to miss perhaps the most significant and hopeful feature of this critical time'.[1] The admission of fallibility makes possible the opening of a genuine dialogue between M.R.A. and the historic Christian Churches. With this may be coupled the concluding sentence of Driberg's book: 'If, then, we can learn from them, perhaps it is not too arrogant to wish that they in turn might, now and then, feel disposed to learn something from us.'

It is, then, in preparation for such a dialogue that it is appropriate for members of the historic Christian Churches to put some questions to M.R.A. This will be attempted in the present chapter in briefest and most direct way in the form of a series of questions asking for further illumination from M.R.A.

1. While acknowledging that truth, honesty, unselfishness and love, are the fruits (though not the only fruits) of the Holy Spirit, do you sufficiently allow for the primacy of the Christian virtue of humility?

2. While rightly acknowledging that the Christian faith and way of life is to be a present possession, do you also stress that there is a Christian hope of everlasting life?

3. While properly confessing that Christianity is the acknowledgment of God's rule and reign in personal life, do you also emphasize that this will also require profound changes in the

---

[1] P. 21. I should have thought the Liturgical Movement, the development of Christian social thinking and action, and the achievements of the Ecumenical Movement (Roman Catholic, Orthodox, Anglican, and Protestant) were far more significant as hopeful signs than seeing 'the Hand of God' in M.R.A.

political, social, and economic structures of society, so that individual patronage shall give way to social justice?

4. While rightly insisting that 'good news' must be proclaimed by word and by transformed life, do you sufficiently distinguish between the commendation of the Gospel because it is true, and the commendation of the Gospel because of its by-products, such as interior security or morale-building?

5. While rightly perceiving that rationality may be the means of denying or postponing the claim of God on human life, do you also fully allow for the place of honest doubt and for the unhampered discussion of theological and sociological perspectives differing from your own official M.R.A. viewpoint?

6. While rightly recognizing the power for good which 'key' people may exercise when 'changed', do you consider that the advertisement of 'success stories' in your official propaganda may not be in accordance with the Gospel precept to avoid ostentation, so that your left hand may not know what your right hand is doing?

7. In rightly recognizing the importance of the 'little church' within the larger Church, have you not underestimated the significance of the theological, liturgical, and ethical traditions of the world-spanning and centuries-transcending Body of Christ of which all present Communions are branches?

8. Can you consistently commend a once Christocentric faith to the West with a merely moral ideology to the East and claim to be Christian in any commonly accepted theological (as contrasted with an ethical) sense? Is it a *theology* or an *ideology* that you ultimately stand for?

It should also be made clear that M.R.A. will have its own questions to ask about the timid, lethargic, custom-bound, and chill levels of Christian obedience in many Communions. These, too, should be welcomed in any genuine attempt at dialogue as the honest prelude to a possible reconciliation.

Further reading

Buchman, Frank D. (speeches), *Remaking the World* (Blandford, London, rev. edn., 1959); *Frank Buchman: Eighty* (Blandford, London, 1959)

Driberg, Tom, *The Mystery of Moral Re-Armament* (Secker and Warburg, London, 1964)

Howard, Peter, *Ideas Have Legs* (Frederick Muller, London, 1945); *Frank Buchman's Secret* (Heinemann, London, 1961)

Marcel, Gabriel (ed.), *Fresh Hope for the World* (Longmans, London, 1960)

Thornton-Duesbery, J. P., *The Oxford Group: A Brief Account of its Principles and Growth* (Moral Re-Armament, London, 1947); *The Open Secret of M.R.A.* (Blandford, London, 1964)

Williamson, Geoffrey, *Inside Buchmanism* (Watts, London, 1954)

5

THE MORMONS

For other foundation can no man lay than that which is laid, which is Jesus Christ. (I Cor. 3.11)

THE MORMONS are so called from the *Book of Mormon*, their official source-book, but prefer to call themselves 'The Church of Jesus Christ of Latter-Day Saints'. This unusual religious society is found chiefly in the United States of America, but, as it is an efficient proselytizing body, its 1,700,000 members are found scattered throughout the British Commonwealth and even as far north as Iceland and as far east as China.

Four factors help to account for the remarkable spread of Mormonism. Chief of these is its militant missionary spirit, which was first shown in 1837 when its ambassadors first reached the shores of England. Every Mormon designated for missionary work by the community is under the latter's absolute orders for two- or four-year periods, during which time he is required to defray his own travelling and sustentation allowances. Such enthusiasm and altruism is infectious. Secondly, Mormons have undoubtedly won many adherents in the United States who were drawn by the saga of Brigham Young's intrepid trek across the Rockies until he reached Salt Lake and there made the desert blossom like the rose. To this day the Mormon State of Utah has a nationwide reputation for its excellence in the fields of public education, health and social services, and its citizens are justly renowned for their industry, sobriety, frugality, honesty and cheerfulness. Thirdly, the Mormon creed is extremely simple and those who embrace it are assured of the support of their fellow 'Saints'. Finally, the

Mormons know the meaning of generosity. In addition to giving a tenth of their income to the Church, they have 'fast offerings' on the first Sunday of each month when they donate the monetary equivalent of the two meals they have gone without for the support of the poor. Several Mormons have held high political office, notably President Eisenhower's Secretary for Agriculture and the present Governor of Michigan.

I

The history of Mormonism is the key to unlock its beliefs. Its founder was Joseph Smith, and its greatest organizer was Brigham Young. Smith was born in the village of Sharon, Vermont, New England, late in 1805. From his parents he inherited credulity and a weak constitution, further enfeebled by epilepsy. His education, as his discipline, was sadly neglected. Indeed, he openly described himself as 'a rough stone, desiring the learning of heaven alone'. At the age of fifteen, he claimed to have seen a vision and received a call to become a 'prophet of the Most High God'. In 1822 he further claimed to have received an angelic messenger who came directly from the Divine Presence. The burden of the message was that he would find a precious religious volume hidden in a hill. He was informed that this volume was written on plates of gold and contained the history of the former inhabitants of the North American Continent and the fullest account of the Gospel as delivered by Christ to the ancient inhabitants. He would be able to interpret this volume with the aid of two crystals, which were the emblems and the instruments of seers and prophets of former ages.

Four years later he claimed that the angel instructed him where to look for the golden volume and that he immediately dug it up. These golden pages were inscribed, he maintained, in fine hieroglyphics which the Mormons have since identified as 'Reformed Egyptian' script. With the aid of the promised crystals, he claimed that he was enabled to translate the hieroglyphics at sight. Our mystification at the linguistic expertness of this barely literate man is increased by the assurance of egyptologists that Egyptian hieroglyphics remained unchanged from the fifth century BC until the fourth century AD. Furthermore, not only is 'Reformed Egyptian' unknown to the egyptologists, but these experts themselves were unable to decipher Egyptian inscriptions until the discovery of the Rosetta stone. We are left to judge between a great illusion and a great miracle, as the explanation of these events.

The English translation of the hieroglyphics, dictated behind a curtain, to scribes, became what is known as the *Book of Mormon*. It was begun at Manchester in 1827 and finished at Fayette, New York State, in 1829. The original manuscript was lost, and only Cowdrey's copy remains. What is much more inconvenient for the enquirer is the disappearance of the original gold volume.

A summary of the contents of the *Book of Mormon* is best given in Smith's words:

We are informed by these records that America in ancient times has been inhabited by two distinct races of people. The first were called Jaredites, and came directly from the Tower of Babel. The second race came directly from the city of Jerusalem about six hundred years before Christ. They were principally Israelites, of the descendants of Joseph. The Jaredites were destroyed about the time that the Israelites came from Jerusalem, who succeeded them in the inhabitance of the country. The principal nation of the second race fell in battle towards the end of the fourth century. The remnant are the *Indians* who now inhabit the country. This book also tells us that Our Saviour also made His appearance upon this continent after His resurrection: that He planted the gospel here in all its fulness and richness, and power and blessing; that they had apostles, prophets, pastors, teachers, evangelists; the same order, the same priesthood, the same ordinances, gifts, powers and blessing as was enjoyed on the Eastern Continent; that the people were cut off in consequence of their transgressions; that the last of their prophets who existed among them was commanded to write an abridgement of their prophecies, history, etc., and to hide it up in the earth, and that it should come forth and be united with the Bible for the accomplishment of the purpose of God in the last days.[1]

[1] Smith's article is printed in I. D. Rupp, *An Original History of the Denominations of the United States* (1844), p. 4.

Thus, Smith's claims as a prophet rest upon a questionable ethnology and dubious history, not to mention that the *Book of Mormon* is to be regarded as a supplement to the Bible and of equal authority.

From being a passive translator, Smith developed into a prophet and legislator with the publication of the *Book of Commandments*, followed by the *Book of Doctrine and Covenants*. These combined an insistence upon the imminence of the Second Advent, with a request to revive the 'charismatic signs' of the primitive Church, including miracles, the gift of tongues, faith-healing, prophecies and continued revelations.

This new religious community became increasingly unpopular, due to its advocacy of polygamy. In consequence, the Mormons were repeatedly obliged to move westwards. The new kingdom of the elect, their 'Zion', was to be Missouri. Thence, after further strenuous objections on the part of their new neighbours, they moved to the vicinity of Commerce in the State of Illinois, where they founded the town of Nauvoo. Here they had to face further persecution, and Smith and his brother were incarcerated in Carthage jail at the request of the Governor. On June 27, 1844, a mob with blackened faces broke into the prison and shot both the brothers. The effect of this murder was to translate Joseph Smith from a leader with a powerful imagination into a martyr in the minds of his followers.

The prophet's mantle fell upon Brigham Young. In 1847 he started for the Rocky Mountains with a selected group of stalwarts. After overcoming Herculean difficulties, they reached the Great Salt Lake and began, with typical industry, to plough up the infertile land and to plant crops on the very spring day of their arrival. In the same autumn 700 wagons arrived at Salt Lake and a year later they were joined by a further thousand wagons. They built a great city and a State of their own as an abiding monument to their faith and industry. Utah was admitted to the comity of the United States in 1895.

II

At first glance, the Mormon creed is that of a simple, evangelical type of Christianity, consisting of three principles: first, faith in God and in Jesus Christ; second, repentance from all sin; and third, baptism for the remission of sin as a preparation for the gift of the Holy Ghost, which is bestowed by the laying-on of hands. Its departure from the norm of historic Christianity can be found in its doctrine of progressive revelations and in the contents of such additional revelations.

The two additions are known as 'baptism for the dead' and 'celestial marriage'. The former is a vicarious baptism undertaken by living Mormons for their dead ancestors who would otherwise miss the joys of heaven. This custom has been acutely described as 'a retro-active application of the Roman Catholic doctrine of purgatory'.[1]

Apart from ordinary marriage vows which last until death, the Mormons allow 'celestial marriage' which is binding beyond death, for they believe that a man will retain all his earthly wives in heaven and beget children there. The custom of 'celestial marriage' may well be a residual part of their former approval of polygamy. Brigham Young certainly both taught and practised polygamy. A conservative estimate is that he married seventeen wives and had forty-seven children by them. He justified the practice on the authority of the example of the patriarchs of the Old Testament and on the need of a large population to exploit the wilderness of Utah. The official defence of the practice was that it enabled a godly man to multiply the creation of a redeemed humanity more rapidly than monogamy would allow. Polygamy is not officially practised today. In fact, Utah was only admitted into the number of the United States in 1895 after its representatives had promised to proscribe polygamy. Some of the cruelty of polygamy was softened by the necessity laid upon every polygamist to obtain both the consent of his previous wife or wives and the sanction of the community, which was dependent upon his economic sufficiency. None the less, it was a custom more suitable to the Old than the New Dispensation. Moreover, even the modified form of polygamy, the 'celestial marriage', contravenes the declaration of our Lord that in heaven there is neither marriage nor giving in marriage.

It was observed earlier that the first principles of Mormon-

[1] 'Saints, Latter Day'—Article by I. W. Riley in Hastings. D.R.E., Vol. XI.

ism are apparently thoroughly evangelical. In fact, however, there are serious departures from orthodox Christian teaching on the nature of God and the person and work of Christ. God is conceived of by them as an exalted man. Furthermore, the Mormon priesthood is declared to be itself the Kingdom of God, and to disobey them is to disobey God.

Not only is the pre-existence of Jesus before His Incarnation denied, but the Gospel records are either contradicted or unwarrantably augmented. He is declared to be 'the son of Adam-God and Mary'. Jesus is further said to have married the Marys and Martha at Cana, thus providing a convenient sanction for Mormon polygamy. Irreverent fantasy can proceed no further than the Mormon assertion that Jesus traced his Davidic descent through David's plural wife Bathsheba, and the unwarrantable conclusion that if David had not been a polygamist, there would have been no Messiah. Furthermore, the Atonement wrought by Christ is limited to the pre-Mormon dispensation. Finally, their complete dissociation from the charitable spirit of our Lord is seen in their categorical declaration that all who are not Latter-Day Saints will be everlastingly damned.

III

Admirable as are many of the ethical qualities of the Mormons and the proselytizing zeal of their 12,000 missionaries, their doctrine must be castigated as perversions of 'the faith once delivered to the saints'.

Their faith is not Christo-centric, for Christ is to them merely a forerunner of Joseph Smith and they have dared even to falsify the Gospel records in order to make the Messiah fit in with their preconceptions. A faith cannot be called 'Christian' with any justice, if it judges the Christ instead of submitting itself to his authority, and if it replaces the 'obedience of faith' by obedience to the dictates of the Mormon hierarchy as the condition of salvation.

The Mormon theory of progressive revelations destroys the finality and the uniqueness of the revelation brought by the incarnate, crucified and risen Lord of history. Indeed, it stands self-condemned by its own mutability. An outstanding example of such convenient divergence is seen in the supersession of the monogamous *Book of Commandments* by the polygamous *Book of Doctrine and Covenants*. The change was dictated, we may surmise, not by a fuller illumination of the Holy Spirit, but by an access of the impulse towards sensuality.

By Old Testament standards (though not by the criteria of the eighth-century prophets), the morality of the Mormons is admirable, but it comes far short of the sacrificial love inculcated in the New Testament. It is a negative, legalistic, even puritanical code. Apart from the unworthy and degrading view of women which polygamy and 'celestial marriage' countenance, it is impossible to forget the utter ruthlessness with which Brigham Young and his 400 'Wolf Hunters' punished the men and women who tried to escape from Salt Lake City in their disillusionment. Furthermore, the autocratic exercise of power by the Mormon hierarchy over the ordinary members is a denial of the liberty of the Christian man and conflicts with our Lord's request to his disciples that they should not exercise authority as the rulers of the Gentiles do, but with the affection of friendship.

There are very great difficulties in accepting the authority of *The Book of Mormon*. There exists no other literature in 'Reformed Egyptian' to match the extra-biblical literature in the languages of the Bible. Further, Nephi, who is said to have engraved the first sacred plates in 'Reformed Egyptian', was a Jew living in Jerusalem about 600 BC when the spoken and written tongue was Hebrew. How could he learn to speak and write 'Reformed Egyptian' in Jerusalem and much more in America? Why an unnecessary miracle for those who spoke Hebrew already? Further, how did Moroni, Joseph Smith's guide, whose language was 'Reformed Egyptian', decipher plates of the Jaredites, allegedly written in language supposedly spoken by Adam and Eve? Are there any extant examples of pre-Columbian gold plates? How can we account for 27,000 words from the King James or Authorized Version of the Bible in Smith's 'translation'? [1]

---

[1] On this complex and tangled matter, see A. Hoekema, *The Four Major Cults* (1963), pp. 75-87; G. B. Arbaugh, *Revelation in Mormonism* (Chicago Univ. Press, 1932); Arthur Budvarson, *The Book of Mormon: True or False?* (Zondervan, Grand Rapids,

Furthermore, neither the character of Smith nor of Young lends credibility to their claims to be prophets. Smith was a bank-note forger and it is improbable that this shifty, illiterate and credulous person would have been remembered but for the murder which made him a martyr. Brigham Young shared his predecessor's sensuality, to which he added his own refinements of cruelty. Neither man had the integrity nor the humility which commonly distinguish the prophets of the living God.

Further reading

The chief original sources are: *The Book of Mormon* (1830), *The Doctrines and Covenants* (1835), and *The Pearl of Great Price* (1851). Also important is *Brigham Young's Discourses*, ed. John A. Widtsoe (Deseret Book Co., Salt Lake City, Utah, 1925). Their history is officially recounted in Joseph Fielding Smith, *Essentials in Church History* (Deseret Book Co., Salt Lake City, Utah, 11th edn., 1946)

Arbaugh, G. B., *Revelation in Mormonism* (University of Chicago Press, Chicago, Illinois, 1932)

Arbaugh, G. B., *Gods, Sex and Saints* (Augustana, Minneapolis, Minnesota, 1957)

Erickson, Ephraim E., *The Psychological and Ethical Aspects of Mormonism* (University of Chicago Press, 1911)

Roberts, B. H. (ed.), *History of the Church of Latter-Day Saints* (6 vols., Salt Lake City, 1902-12)

Whalen, William J., *The Latter-Day Saints in the Modern Day World: An Account of Contemporary Mormonism* (John Day, U.S.A., 1964)

Michigan); and, from the Mormon side, Milton R. Hunter, *Archaeology and the Book of Mormon* (Vol. I, Deseret Book Co., Salt Lake City, Utah, 1956) and Francis W. Kirkham, *A New Witness for Christ in America* (2 vols., Zion's Press, Independence, 1951).

6

JEHOVAH'S WITNESSES

But now abideth faith, hope and charity; and the greatest of these is charity. (I Cor. 13.13)

JEHOVAH'S WITNESSES is the final name chosen by a sect which has been known variously as 'The Millennial Dawn', 'The International Bible Students Association', 'The Watchtower Organization', and the company of those who subscribe to the doctrine 'Millions now living will never die!' The present designation of this body was applied to it by 'Judge' Rutherford in 1931 and is based upon the words of the prophet, 'Ye are my witnesses, saith Jehovah'.[1] This prolific group has come into the public eye by reason of its pertinacious tractsellers and because its adherents refuse to accept military service or blood transfusion. In 1952 there were 13,492 congregations of which 3,103 were to be found in the United States and 695 in the British Isles. According to *The Yearbook of Jehovah's Witnesses* (1964) their membership in the United States in 1963 was 308,370.

I

It originated in the mind of Charles Taze Russell at Alleghany, Pittsburgh, in 1872. Its author, then aged twenty, was a member of the local Congregational Church and of the Y.M.C.A. in the neighbourhood. The real forerunners of the movement, however, were a group of Second Adventists, and in particular, a J. H. Paton to whose writings Russell was greatly indebted, though it was beneath him to acknowledge this.

[1] Isa. 43.10.

Russell was a wealthy haberdasher, who had inherited five shops from his father, but which he sold in order to devote his entire working days to the dissemination of his views. As a speaker he was compelling, and as an organizer efficient. In 1874 he founded a new religious organization named the Zion's Watch Tower Society. Apart from a magazine which he edited and largely wrote, and a mass of tracts which he composed, he produced a seven volume series entitled *Studies in the Scriptures*, which is the main compendium of the doctrines of the Witnesses. The movement spread to England in 1880 and in a further eight years its representatives were active in China, India, Turkey, Haiti and Africa.

Russell is a curiously disreputable figure to have originated a new religious movement. So overweening was his egotism that he claimed to be a competent Greek scholar, though, as was proved in court, he did not know a letter of the alphabet of that language. His domineering conceit and wayward affections became widely known when his wife sued him for divorce and her petition was readily granted. He was accused by the *Brooklyn Eagle* of selling grain, which he advertised as 'miracle-wheat', at sixty dollars a bushel, and he admitted that there was 'some element of truth' in the charge. He was also believed to have played upon the fears of sick persons to induce them to make over their fortunes to his organization. This was all the more hypocritical of him as he jibed at the moneys collected by the Christian Churches and advertised Witness gatherings as 'No Collection Meetings'. His egotism was boundless, for he stated in the introductory pages of his *Studies in the Scriptures* that it would be better to leave the Bible unopened and to read his commentary on it, than to omit the latter and read only the Bible.

Russell died in October 1916. So impressed was the attorney of the Witnesses, the misnamed 'Judge' Rutherford, that he wrote:

When the history of the Church of Christ is fully written, it will be found that the place next to St. Paul in the gallery of fame as expounders of the Gospel of the great Master will be occupied by Charles Taze Russell.[1]

[1] Cited by H. H. Stroup, *The Jehovah's Witnesses* (Columbia University Press, 1945), pp. 12-13.

It is hardly surprising that so ardent a devotee of the founder of the movement should have been elected to succeed him. From 1917 until his death in 1942, Rutherford led the Witnesses with an iron but successful hand. He, too, was a prolific writer and he implemented the propaganda of the organization by a radio network and the sale of gramophone records of his addresses. In 1942 Nathan Knorr succeeded Rutherford.

Despite its popularity, however, the movement was banned in several countries because its adherents refused the duties of citizenship and proselytized amongst the members of the Christian Churches. They were proscribed in Northern Rhodesia, after a disturbance in the Copper Belt in the nineteen-thirties. In 1940 and 1941 the New Zealand and Australian Governments outlawed them as a subversive organization. In January 1947 the Supreme Court of Canada ruled that they 'were not a religious body' and in the same year they were banned in Southern Rhodesia. About 6,000 of them suffered in Hitler's concentration camps.[1]

II

One of the main reasons for their success in terms of statistics is their autocratic and hierarchic type of organization. This is marked by all the efficiency characteristic of a modern international business-house. At the head is a central, all-powerful Board of Directors. Under this Board and responsible to it are the various 'Religious Servants' and beneath them the many 'Circuit Servants'. Below them are the 'District Servants', and the 'Branch Servants' below the latter. Local groups are known as 'Congregations', each of which meets in a 'Kingdom Hall' overseen by a 'Congregational Servant'. He is assisted by a 'service committee' which takes charge of various activities, particularly of the 'back calls', that is, repeated visiting of contacts. Women are discouraged from seeking office and each member of the hierarchy obeys the orders of his superior without question.

The chief task of the Witnesses is the distribution of the official publications from door to door. Each member is ex-

[1] Royston Pike, *Jehovah's Witnesses* (Watts, London, and Philosophical Library, New York, 1954), p. 26.

pected to assume his share of these duties and many are equipped with a portable gramophone on which recordings of Rutherford's sermons are played to the householders. All details of visits have to be reported on specially printed forms to the Board of Directors at headquarters. In brief, the Witnesses are organized as a group of religious commercial travellers.

A survey of their teaching will reveal that the Jehovah's Witnesses are heretics, in addition to being schismatics. In their doctrine of God they are monotheistic, if not definitely unitarian. Perhaps their teaching about the person of Christ is most akin to the Arian heresy of the fourth century AD, for they assert that the Son of God is a created being. This is the purport of the following citation from Russell:

> As he (Jesus) was the highest of all Jehovah's creation, so also was he the first, the direct creation of God, the 'only Begotten', and then he, as Jehovah's power, and in his name, created all things. . . .[1]

Russell repudiates the Chalcedonian Definition's claim that in Jesus Christ the divine and human natures co-existed:

> Neither was Jesus a combination of the two natures, human and spiritual. The blending of two natures produces neither the one nor the other, but an imperfect, hybrid thing, which is obnoxious to the divine arrangement.[2]

The Witnesses are committed to the curious belief that before his incarnation Jesus was the Archangel Michael, which they believe is taught in Dan. 12.1. They also hold that Jesus gave up his angelic nature in the days of his flesh and was an ordinary fallible mortal. They claim that, although Jesus was not divine, he paid at his death the ransom necessary to set men free from death, but that his work of Atonement 'will be completed with the close of the Millennial Age'.[3] They further reduce the stature of the eternal Son of God by declaring that

[1] *Studies in the Scriptures*, V, p. 84.
[2] *Ibid.*, I, p. 179.
[3] J. K. van Baalen, *The Chaos of Cults* (Eerdmans, Grand Rapids, Michigan, 1938), p. 147. See also Pike, *op. cit.*, p. 37.

elect Christians, 'the little flock', will 'be reckoned as joint
sacrificers, joint mediators, joint reconcilers' with Jesus.[1] Salvation largely consists in being imitators of Jesus, which argues,
of course, self-salvation.

The Witnesses do not believe that the redeeming work of
Christ was completed on the Cross or that those who have
faith in him are saved from their sins and inherit eternal life.
Russell taught

> The 'ransom for all' given by 'the man Christ Jesus' does
> not give or guarantee everlasting life or blessing to any man;
> but it does guarantee to every man another opportunity or
> trial for life everlasting.[2]

Thus, far from being saved by Christ, each man must work
out his own salvation:

> Some have been blinded in part, and some completely, by
> the God of this world, and they must be recovered from
> blindness as well as from death, that they, *each for himself*,
> may have a full chance to prove, by obedience or disobedi-
> ence, their worthiness or unworthiness of life eternal.[3]

This is clearly justification by works, not justification by
faith.

The Witnesses also believe that Jesus was provided with a
new spiritual body at the resurrection, and that his human body
was neither raised nor glorified. In one place Russell teaches:

> He was put to death *a man*, but was raised from the dead
> a *spirit being* of the highest order of the divine nature . . .[4]

In another he declares:

> Our Lord's human body was, however, supernaturally
> removed from the tomb; because had it remained there it
> would have been an insurmountable obstacle to the faith of
> the disciples, who were not yet instructed in spiritual
> things . . .[5]

---

[1] *Ibid.*   [2] *Studies in the Scriptures*, I, p. 150.
[3] *Ibid.*, I, p. 158.   [4] *Ibid.*, V, p. 453.   [5] *Ibid.*, II, p. 129.

Significantly (for the Witnesses are essentially a commercial organization), the permanent status of the Ascended Christ is described as being 'the Chief Executive Officer of Jehovah'.[1]

It is not surprising that the Witnesses find the doctrine of the Trinity irrational, since they have reduced the status of the eternal Son of God to that of a fallible mortal and conceive of the Holy Spirit as merely the invisible influence of Jehovah.[2]

They have a ghoulish fondness for the text, 'The wages of sin is death'. They claim that all men are destroyed in death, but that all the dead will be raised again and given a second chance at the Second Advent of Christ. In making such assertions they ignore the promise made by our Lord to the penitent thief, 'This day thou shalt be with me in Paradise', and the implications of the metaphor by which the New Testament describes the dead as those 'that are fallen asleep in Christ'. The doctrine of the second chance is an encouragement to libertarians, apart from its infidelity to the New Testament insistence on the way of salvation and the way of damnation as irrevocable destinies of men. This doctrine alone gives substance to the taunt that the teaching of the Jehovah's Witnesses is the religion of the natural man. Should evil men refuse the proffered salvation the second time, their fate will be annihilation, not eternal torment or damnation.

Despite the erroneous nature of much of this teaching the Witnesses can be congratulated on refusing to picture God as a divine sadist, whose dignity is established by the torturing of the damned. Rutherford taught:

Eternal torture is void of the principle of love, 'God is love'. A Creator that would torture His creatures eternally would be a fiend, and not a God of love.[3]

Furthermore, the Witnesses teach that even death may be spiritually remedial. Their weakness is that they cannot conceive of divine love as *holy* love also: a world without rewards and punishments here and hereafter would be an immoral universe.

The unscriptural speculation of the Witnesses is given full scope in their account of the Second Advent and the Millen-

[1] *Ibid.*, p. 188. [2] Rutherford, *Riches*, p. 94.
[3] *World Distress*, p. 40.

nium. Russell declared that the Seventh Millennium was the beginning of the Reign of Christ, and he calculated that 1872 was the exact six-thousandth year from the Creation of Adam and Eve. He prophesied that the final end of the world would take place in 1914. Since that time his followers have postponed the date to some time before 1984 when Gabriel's trumpet will blow and Christ will announce that the final end has come. Then God's 'Great Theocracy' will be established on earth and Jehovah's Witnesses will be the only survivors to share in this Divine Kingdom.

Their account of the Millennium is far more detailed than that offered by the Book of Revelation and they have already decided how the problem of feeding the resurrected bodies may be solved:

> Remembering the Lord's promise that in the Millennial period 'the earth shall yield her increase' and that the desert and the wilderness-places of the earth shall become as a Garden of Eden, we may safely estimate upon all the land, which we may find, according to recent estimates, to be 57,000,000 square miles or over 36,000,000,000 acres. What would this mean as to space for each individual who has ever lived in the world, i.e. 28,441,126,838 persons? It means that there would be twelve-hundred and seventy-five acres for each little village of two hundred families. Quite a sufficiency of room, all will agree, under the new conditions promised. But if more space be necessary, with faith we will readily see that it will be quite within the divine power to raise vast continents from the depths of the ocean, or indeed to give a literal as well as a symbolical fulfilment to the declaration— 'There shall be no more sea.'[1]

The only fitting retort to such speculations is that of Dr Reinhold Niebuhr, that faith has nothing to do with either the furniture of heaven or the temperature of hell!

After the battle of Armageddon the 144,000 faithful Jehovah's Witnesses will be taken up into heaven, there to rule with Christ over the new earth, which will be inhabited by the Jonadabs, or people of good will.

In our account of the beliefs of the Witnesses we cannot omit their loveless condemnation of the Christian Churches as

[1] Rutherford, *Riches*, p. 188.

devil-controlled. There could be no worse offence against
Christian charity than this typical citation from their teaching:

> These facts are set forth here, not for the purpose of hold-
> ing men up to ridicule, but for the purpose of informing the
> people that the ecclesiastical systems, Catholic and Protest-
> ant, are under supervision and control of the Devil, and form
> a part of his visible organization, and therefore constitute the
> anti-Christ.[1]

A group claiming to be Christian, yet so vicious in its attitude to others who take the name of Christ on their lips, is
guilty of an inner contradiction, for its spirit denies its profession.

In general, Jehovah's Witnesses fall under censure on four
main characteristics. First, their doctrine is based upon an
arbitrary selection of texts from the Scriptures, but the main
body of the teaching of Jesus and his apostles is either evaded
or perverted; and to each ounce of the Bible a hundredweight
of speculation is added.

In the second place, their doctrine is largely based upon the
obscurities of such apocalyptic books as Daniel and Revelation, implying that the Revelation of God is a tangled skein
only to be unravelled by the subtle minds of this sect. But
Christianity is not a mystery religion for initiates, for we 'have
seen the glory of God in the face of Jesus Christ', who declared 'I am the light of the world'.

Thirdly, the use of the Bible as an *Old Moore's Almanac* of
prediction is to misunderstand its purpose and to claim to know
more than our Lord himself who confessed that he did not
know the time of the coming of the Son of Man again on the
clouds.

Fourthly, their creed must be rejected because it offers salvation on too easy terms, affirming, in effect, that payment for
it may be deferred to another existence. This is to repudiate
the solemn and urgent either-or of the Bible, and to senti-
mentalize the conception of a Holy God. Moreover, as we have
seen, this is a salvation by good works, not by faith in the
victory of Christ. This is proven by the fact that only the

[1] Rutherford, *Deliverance*, p. 222. In *Creation* Rutherford referred to 'pious frauds, called preachers or clergymen'.

worthy few are admitted to the single annual celebration of the Lord's Supper to receive the elements. In 1951, for instance, 623,760 Witnesses attended, but only 21,619 partook of the Supper.[1]

III

One further question remains to be answered: How have the devotees of such an unbalanced creed succeeded in winning so many members? This question is merely another way of asking: What can the Churches learn from the strategy of Jehovah's Witnesses?

Russell's success was partly due to his clarity of thought, simplicity of expression in untechnical language, and abundance of illustrations drawn from everyday life. Further, he and his followers have an unrivalled knowledge of Holy Writ and can quote chapter and verse for their opinions. It has been established that there are over 5,000 different scriptural citations in the books of Russell.[2] Jehovah's Witnesses have had the wisdom to assume and count upon every member being a propagandist of its organization, using the most up-to-date methods such as gramophone and radios and attractively printed, bound and illustrated volumes.

Even their doctrines, in at least two cases, represent a healthy protest and reaction against current Christian orthodoxy. In their teaching about the 'last things' they refuse to accept the 'fire and brimstone' picture of Hell and rightly protest against a doctrine that envisages punishment as vindictive, not remedial. The Jehovah's Witnesses, although denying the responsibilities of citizenship in so many ways, have protested against the devilries of modern warfare and the extravagance of modern life. It is also on record that their egalitarian convictions impelled them to welcome Socialism even in its early days, when few religious folk were Socialists. These, even when we condemn the Jehovah's Witnesses in so much, must be counted as its assets.

Their strongest asset, however, is the capacity for sacrifice. H. H. Stroup, an objective observer, says of them: 'They are willing to give up friends and family, to work indefatigably, to

---

[1] Royston Pike, *Jehovah's Witnesses*, p. 117.
[2] Cf. J. Black, *New Forms of the Old Faith*, p. 200.

give unstintingly of their money, to withstand bitter persecution, and even, in certain European countries, to remain loyal to their convictions unto death . . .'[1]

Further reading

Bates, E. S., Article on 'Russell, Charles Taze' in *Dictionary of American Biography* (1931)

Pike, Royston, *Jehovah's Witnesses* (Watts, London, and Philosophical Library, New York, 1954)

Rutherford, 'Judge': his chief works are: *Religion, Salvation, Enemies, Riches, Light, Government, Prophecy, Reconciliation, Preservation, Deliverance, The Harp of God,* and *Preparation.* His most important pamphlets are perhaps *Theocracy, Armageddon* and *God and the State*

Stroup, H. H., *The Jehovah's Witnesses* (Columbia University Press, New York, 1945)

The Yearbook of the Jehovah's Witnesses, published annually since 1933, gives a useful account of the worldwide activities of the Witnesses

[1] *The Jehovah's Witnesses,* p. 63.

7

BRITISH-ISRAEL

> *. . . the Gentiles are fellow-heirs, and fellow-members of the body, and fellow-partakers of the promise in Jesus Christ through the gospel.* (Eph. 3.6)

> *I perceive God is no respecter of persons.* (Acts 10.34)

> *There is neither Jew nor Greek . . . Ye are all one man in Christ Jesus. And if ye are Christ's, then ye are Abraham's seed, heirs according to the promise.*
> (Gal. 3.28-9)

BRITISH-ISRAEL is a theory, rather than a sect or heresy, held by some two million adherents within the Protestant Communions. British-Israelites hold that the British Commonwealth of Nations and the United States of America are the descendants of the ten lost tribes of Israel and that they inherit today the political promises made by God to ancient Israel. This theory, like many of the tenets of the sects, is based upon highly fanciful exegesis of the Bible.

Protestants have been rightly termed 'the People of a Book'. This was expressed most cogently by Chillingworth when he claimed: 'The Bible and the Bible alone is the religion of Protestants.' Today it would be desirable to amend this definition to indicate that the Bible was the *basis* of the religion of Protestants. When Martin Luther dared to criticize the corruptions of the later medieval Church in the West, his only authority was 'The Word of God'. This alone, he claimed, was an authority higher than the Church. He therefore demanded a 'Reformation according to the Word of God'. Protestants stand proudly within this great tradition and are thus obliged to measure all policies by 'the rule of faith' in the Holy Scriptures. Our faith, our ethics, our liturgy, are inescapably biblical.

If the Bible is, in fact, the sole doctrinal authority of Protestants, why are there so many sects amongst Protestants? Here the term 'sects' is to be distinguished from 'denominations' because the latter accept the Scriptures as the supreme rule of faith and life, and differ radically only in their various forms of ecclesiastical government. By the 'sects' is intended the congeries of bodies which have seceded or broken away from the historic Christian Churches to establish their own organizations in opposition. Among a vast and variegated array which includes the Seventh-Day Adventists, Jehovah's Witnesses, Mormons and Russellites, the 'sects' witness to the danger of biblical exegesis uninfluenced by the traditional wisdom and experience of the Church of the centuries. When once the Bible was issued to the people translated into their native tongues, without assistance in its interpretation, they misunderstood parts of it, ignored other sections of it, and often read into it their presuppositions or prejudices. The anthology of the Bible thus compiled by subjectivism was erected into a variety of religious systems for which the authority of the biblical record was claimed.

Such, then, was the peril of private and idiosyncratic interpretation of the Scriptures. Equally hazardous was the exclusively literal exegesis of the Scriptures. Unfortunately, this danger does not only beset those outside the historic Christian Churches; it is often found within them. An instance of ingenious private interpretation, literalist in type, may be given here. Sir James Young Simpson, the distinguished Scottish surgeon, was once thwarted in his attempts to introduce chloroform into gynaecology by a group of 'fundamentalist' ministers of religion, who urged the authority of the Creation text, 'In sorrow and labour shalt thou bring forth thy children'. His retort out-literalized the literalists, by claiming that he had divine authority in the same narrative for the use of anaesthetics, for God had put Adam 'into a deep sleep' before removing his rib. This apparent digression is relevant to the study of British-Israel, for this is a theory based upon private and often crassly literalist misinterpretations of the Bible.

I

The claims of British-Israelitism must now be considered. The necessary information on the principles of the British-Israel World Federation may be found in two of their authoritative compilations. One is a pamphlet by Commander Studd, entitled *Britain's Place in Prophecy*, and the other, *The Heritage of the Anglo-Saxon Race*, by M. H. Gayer, O.B.E.

From a perusal of these expositions, it appears that British-Israelites hold three basic beliefs. Firstly, they maintain that the Old Testament prophecies made by God to Abraham and confirmed to his descendants must be literally and materially fulfilled. In the second place, they hold that these promises and subsequent prophecies require for their fulfilment a belief that the ten tribes of the northern kingdom of Israel must have persisted as a nation, ruled by a king of the Davidic dynasty. Thirdly, they claim that Britain, the British Empire, and the United States of America, are the inheritors of the promises of God because they are the descendants of the ten lost tribes of Israel, and because Britain is ruled by a monarch of the Davidic line.

The last hypothesis they attempt to establish in an ingenious, if unconvincing, manner. The ten tribes, they maintain, were taken captive by the Assyrians in the eighth century BC. From captivity they wandered over Europe as the Scythians, Cimmerians, and Goths. From Europe they invaded England as the Angles, Saxons, Jutes and Normans, commingling their blood with that of the Ancient Britons. Therefore, they insist, the citizens of Britain, the British Commonwealth and the Americans, are the inheritors of the divine promises to Abraham and constitute the New Israel, the master-nation. A summary of this fanciful reconstruction of ethnology is provided by one of their own writers:

> Getae, Massagetae, Sacae, Scythians, Goths, Ostro-Goths, Dacians, Khumri, Milesians, Danes, Jutes, Angles, Saxons, Normans—with many another name that could be added—all at last, either by trade or simple migration, but mostly by fierce fighting and conquest the one or the other found their way into these 'Isles of the West'. They were 'sifted among the nations', as God said they would be, but not a 'grain'

has been lost, and out of them all have truly evolved the English, Scotch, Irish, Welsh of the British Empire, and the American of the United States.[1]

If their ethnology is fanciful, their philology is fantastic! 'Saxon' is interpreted as 'Saac's sons' and therefore means Isaac's sons, thus fulfilling God's promise of Genesis 21.12: 'In Isaac shall thy seed be called.' No less far-fetched is the derivation of 'British' from *berithish, berith* being the Hebrew for 'covenant' and *ish* the Hebrew for 'man', i.e. men of the covenant. Fantasy goes even further in claiming that 'John Bull' was so named because Isaac's British sons sacrificed the bullock, which in Hebrew is spelled *engle*, hence 'England'.[2]

The foundation-stone of the entire edifice of British-Israel is the belief that the promises and prophecies of the Old Testament must be fulfilled literally. Otherwise, it is suggested, God is made to appear a liar and a breaker of his Word. One important point, however, seems to be ignored. That is, that nowhere in his Word does God declare that his promises are to be fulfilled to the letter. It is, in fact, quite impossible to discover a literal meaning in much of the Scriptures. Why, therefore, should the promises be interpreted literally and not metaphorically? Scripture has not always a simple, straightforward meaning, any more than everyday speech has.

One instance of the folly of interpreting common parlance literally may be given, for in this respect God's parlance (the Word of God) is analogous. Let us suppose that a young man has recently become engaged, and that his ecstasy finds expression in a love-letter by a quotation from a lyric. He writes to his fiancée that 'My love is like a red, red rose'. He does not imply by this description that she is a ruddy-cheeked country lass with a florid complexion. Nor is this a subtle way of declaring that she is lovely, but her loveliness will fade and wither with the years. Least of all does he mean that her apparently sweet disposition has unsuspected cruelty lurking beneath it, as thorns below the rose. His meaning (or rather *one* of the layers of meaning) is that as the rose is lovely, so is she. The meaning is metaphorical not literal.

[1] L. Sapsworth, *The Bible Arch of British-Israel Truth*, p. 94.
[2] Ralph Lord Roy, *Apostles of Discord* (Beacon Press, Boston, 1953), p. 96.

The Bible frequently used this metaphorical, short-hand type of speech—these implicit similes. For instance, our Lord says, 'I am the light of the world'. This cannot mean that he is the sun, but that his Person and Message bring illumination to the souls of men darkened by sin. When he says, 'I am the door', it cannot be interpreted as meaning that the composition of his body is wood. His meaning is that, as a door gives entry to a house, so does he open the Kingdom of Heaven to all believers.

The same test should be applied to the promises of God to Abraham and his seed. One example of over-facile British-Israelite exegesis may be considered. God made the following promise to Jacob: 'I will multiply thy seed as the sand which is upon the sea-shore.' The following is Commander Studd's interpretation of this passage:

> They were to be numerous as sand of the sea, suggesting at least a great sea-faring nation.[1]

Does the text suggest that Israel shall be a sea-faring nation? There is not a hint of it. In addition, it seems that Israel had no trace of sea-fever in its history, for when Solomon built a port to the north of the Gulf of Akaba for his joint mercantile enterprises with Hiram, the Phoenician ruler, his fleet had to be manned with Tyrian sailors. The text simply asserts that Jacob's descendants shall be as numerous as the grains of sand upon the sea-shore. The prophetic 'hint' of a sea-faring nation originates in the noble Commander's fertile brain, not in the Bible. We might suggest that the Commander is viewing the Scriptures through the telescope of the Royal Navy; it is even possible that, like Nelson, he puts a blind eye to the telescope! This is but one apposite example of exegesis that fails by literalizing a metaphor.

Two other texts which are used for 'sanctified imperialism' of the British variety are Jer. 25.22, 'the isle beyond the sea', which is interpreted as meaning Britain; and it is said that the promise made to Abraham in Gen. 22.17, 'Thy seed shall possess the gate of his enemies', refers particularly to the British possessions of Gibraltar, Malta, Cyprus and Suez! In fact the literal meaning of the word translated as 'isle' in the

[1] *Britain's Place in Prophecy*, p. 6.

former citation is, as the marginal reading in the Revised Version indicates, 'coastland', and the word translated as 'gates' in the latter citation is simply 'cities'. Clearly, this is exegetical ignorance masquerading as originality.

Such fanciful exegesis must be censured, but it does not dispose of the larger questions: How were the promises to Abraham and his seed fulfilled? The New Testament, nevertheless, does dispose of this question in several places. It claims that the promises and prophecies made by God to the chosen people are fulfilled in Jesus Christ and his community, the New Israel. St Paul, for example, declares: 'The Gentiles are fellow-heirs and fellow-members of the body, and fellow-partakers of the promise in Christ Jesus through the Gospel.' Elsewhere, referring to our Lord, St Paul writes, 'In him are all the promises of God'. In yet another place he states categorically, 'And if ye are Christ's, then are ye Abraham's seed, heirs according to the promise'.

St Peter may also be summoned as a witness to the truth that the promises of God to Abraham are fulfilled in the Christian Church. He says, in a sermon preached to the Jews but with an eye on the Gentiles, 'Ye are the children of the prophets, and of the covenant which God made with our fathers, saying unto Abraham, And in thy seed shall all the families of the earth be blessed. Unto you *first* God, having raised up his Son Jesus, sent him to bless you, in turning every one of you from his iniquities' (Acts 3.25-6). Clearly it is the Church which inherited the fulfilment of the promises in Christ. The Church had comparatively few converts from Judaism, but many Gentiles within its fold. The fulfilment of the promises was not biologically conceived, as the British-Israelities claim it ought to have been. It was a spiritual fulfilment. Since the majority of the chosen people rejected Jesus the Messiah, they had forfeited the promises.

Because these promises were spiritually fulfilled in Christ and conveyed to his faithful followers, regardless of nationality or race, it is unnecessary to look for any biological fulfilment. This being the case, the second and third principles of British-Israel are ruled out of court. Since the promises were spiritually fulfilled and are available for all Christians, it is superfluous to search for evidence of the history of the lost ten tribes of

Israel. Because the fulfilment of Abraham's promises has taken place in the Kingdom of God over which Christ rules as King of kings and Lord of lords, we need not look to the future for the realization of the divine promises to Abraham.

II

If the biblical interpretation of the British-Israelites is eccentric and their re-writing of history chimerical, how can their appeal be accounted for? Several factors play an important part in the attraction of British-Israel. First, it appeals to patriotic people, who find a biblical warrant for the importance of their nation in the affairs of the world. One might go further and say that it is peculiarly attractive to those who believe themselves to be the *Herrenvolk*.

Secondly, it appeals to persons perplexed by the maze of history, who are searching for a philosophy of history which will counteract the apparent insignificance of individuals on the modern scene. To such the Bible offers a key to world-history.

In the third place, they are unconsciously seeking for an adequate doctrine of the Church as the New Israel of God, believing that God calls peoples, not merely individual units, into his service.

This three-fold appeal is a solemn warning for the Churches. They must be more careful to instruct their charges that the international and interracial Church of Christ has claims that override even patriotism. The Churches must learn from the idiosyncratic exegesis of the British-Israelites the need for sounder biblical instruction. It seems, in Professor J. R. Coates's phrase, that many within the Churches look upon the Word of God 'as a sort of time-table in cypher'.[1] Christians are particularly ignorant of the philosophy of the apocalyptic books of the Bible, which are such a happy hunting-ground for sectarians and schismatics.

III

A detailed critique of British-Israel must now be offered. Our first criticism is that, since New Testament days, the need

[1] *Expository Times*, Vol. LIV, p. 315.

for an elect nation has disappeared, for it has been met by the
international Church of Christ. The final Word of God in the
New Testament is that racial distinctions are irrelevant in
the matter of salvation. There is no suggestion in it that there
can be a master-race. Christ's great mission to the world will
be fulfilled by individuals nurtured in community who will
gather up other individuals to whom they have proclaimed the
Gospel into communities. Such individuals and communities
created and confirmed by the Gospel, whatever the race or
races included in their membership, are Christ's chosen people,
the Church.

Christ is Messiah of all nations alike, and as all nations may
be chosen, there is no need for a particular chosen nation. In
the redeemed community or race all distinctions of nationality,
class, race, sex and culture are transcended, for 'there is neither
Jew nor Greek, circumcision nor uncircumcision, Barbarian,
Scythian, bond nor free: but Christ is all in all'. The re-
nascence of doctrines of a privileged race have proved in recent
times dangerous to the peace of the nations, and a poison in
the veins of the Body of Christ, the Church. Such teaching, it
cannot be too often insisted upon, is a flat denial of the Gospel
doctrine. It disregards the words of John the Baptist, 'begin
not to say within yourselves, We have Abraham to our father'.
It refuses to consider seriously St Paul's saying, 'he is not a
Jew which is one outwardly'. It contradicts outright the solemn
declaration of our Lord himself, 'the flesh profiteth nothing'.

It could also be pointed out that the British-Israelites entirely
misunderstand the nature of 'election' even in the Old Covenant, for God chose the Israelites for service, not for privilege.
This was the bitter reminder of the prophecy of Amos, 'You
only have I known of all the families of the earth: therefore I
will visit upon you all your iniquities.' In the deepest thought
of the Old Testament the doctrine of election was expanded
in its charity to include universalism: 'Are ye not as the children of the Ethiopians unto me, O children of Israel? saith the
Lord. Have not I brought up Israel out of the land of Egypt,
and the Philistines from Caphtor, and the Syrians from Kir?'
(Amos 9.7). The British-Israelites are anachronisms.

In the second place, they must be accused of imperfectly
understanding the nature and authority of the Bible, as their

faulty exegesis proves. Whether they deal with the Law, the Prophets, the Writings, the Gospels or the Epistles, they place them on the same level as instructors in Christian doctrine. The Old Testament is more important to them than the New, with the exception of the Book of Revelation. The inspiration of the Bible is not all on the same level: the Bible itself is, in Luther's phrase, the 'cradle of Christ' and the Old Testament must be judged by the Revelation of the Word of God Incarnate, the mind of Christ.

They must be censured for regarding the prophets as prediction-experts. The prophets did not come among the people to foretell distant events; they were there to foretell God's will for their own generation. This distinction is admirably made by Professor J. E. McFadyen in *The Bible and Modern Thought*:

> No one who reads such a book as Amos could carry away the impression that its importance lay in prediction. Running through it, doubtless, is the broad announcement that national sin will issue in national ruin, but the value of this lies in its moral interpretation of history, not in its miraculously predictive quality.

Furthermore, British-Israelite exegesis unwarrantably distinguishes between the fulfilment of passages referring to Israel and those referring to Judah. We may well ask: why should the divine promises made to the whole people apply only to the relatively small segment of the nation which was carried into capitivity?

In the third place, the whole import and emphasis of British-Israel leads to a false sense of racial security, to a dangerous racial pride and an unworthy conception of God. Of this implication of their teaching Dr James Black has said:

> British-Israel theory . . . is dangerously like some modern theories of race superiority which have only brought sorrow, shame and insolence into men's hearts. Quite seriously, I regard this type of idea as one of the dangers to human peace and sanity.[1]

[1] *New Forms of the Old Faith*, p. 282.

Fourthly and finally, it must be stated that the subsidiary historical, ethnological and philological arguments used by the champions of British-Israel are contrary to the ascertained facts and are often fantastically improbable. No reputable archaeologist would be found to agree that the Scythians were of Semitic origin as there are no traces of Semitic influence on either their language or their customs. The ethnological link in the British-Israelite historical chain is so weak that Israel's most distinctive customs—circumcision, seventh-day observance, ritual cleanness—have not survived amongst the Scythians, Cimmerians, Angles, Saxons or Celts. We are informed that the languages of the United Kingdom contain many words akin to Hebrew, but a glance at the *Concise Oxford Dictionary* would explode the delightful philological balloons. Expert philologists assure us that there are no possible links in vocabulary, grammar or syntax between the Semitic language of the ten tribes and the Low or High German of the Teutons.

The crux of the whole theory is historical. But many other claims for the lost ten tribes have been made. The Mormons urge that the Indians of North America are they, while other peoples that have been suggested for the same role are the Laplanders and the Mexicans. The joint editor of Valentine's *Jewish Encyclopedia* maintains that there are only two claims for descent from the lost tribes which have any serious basis, namely those of the Afghans and the Nestorians.

IV

It would be unsatisfactory to let the matter end there. With the British-Israelites we must also recognize that God fulfils his purpose through nations as well as through individuals, though it is the individuals which determine the character of a nation. God's judgments are made known in the arena of history. Nations, as well as individuals, may be the instruments of the divine justice punishing aggressors. The Old Testament indicates that God may anoint nations other than his chosen people Israel, to be the instruments of judgment on his chosen but impenitent people. For this reason Elijah could speak of Hazael, whom he anointed as king of Syria, as God's agent; similarly, but in more direct fashion, a later prophet could speak of the king of Persia, as seen by God, in the following words: 'Thus saith the Lord to his anointed, to Cyrus . . . I will gird thee though thou hast not known me' (Isa. 45.1). Isaiah (10.5) says, 'O Assyrian, the rod of my anger . . .' implying that God's will is made effectual through other nations of the world. Similarly, the dark signature of divine displeasure was written over the ruined cities of Europe. But the nations whom God selects to fulfil his purposes are never master-races; they are servant-races—they exist in order to obey the behests of the Almighty. It is an election to responsibility and even to suffering, as Israel knew of old. No nation is elected by God to lord it over other peoples, as a *Herrenvolk* or imperial régime.

In this strictly limited sense, when to suffer oppression would be worse than to draw the bloody sword of justice, nations may be the agents of divine justice, though never as self-appointed agents. Nations as well as individuals can fall a prey to hypocrisy and Pharisaism. In this sense also, nations that inherit the traditions of a Christian civilization—the so-called 'Christian countries'—are under obligation to protect and perpetuate the Christian faith, and are thus elected.

But the Bible speaks of another sword, more effectual than the sword of justice; it is the Sword of the Spirit, the Word of God. This alone will provide the basis for communal and international integration. Justice is founded upon the threat of coercion, but the Sword of the Spirit is love. Men can be cowed into terror by the sword of justice or war, and when men and nations neglect or spurn the rights of individuals and of other nations, the last recourse of the defenders of divine justice may be this ugly weapon of fear. But lasting unity among the nations becomes possible only when men see the love of God in the Cross of Christ stooping to conquer, embracing man in his loathsomeness and setting him on his feet again. Such divine reconciliation is the only enduring basis of international comity.

The Christian's task is therefore to vanquish the rebellious hearts of men by the weakest thing in the world—the wounds of a crucified King. But the weakness of God is stronger than the power of men, as his folly is wiser than the sagacity of men.

Further reading

Allen, J. H., *Judah's Sceptre and Joseph's Birthright* (Destiny Publishers, 13th edn., 1917)

Gayer, M. H., *The Heritage of the Anglo-Saxon Race* Destiny Publishers, Haverhill, Massachusetts, 1941)

8

CHRISTIAN SCIENCE

*Who in the days of his flesh, having offered up prayers
and supplications with strong crying and tears . . .
though he was a Son, yet learned obedience by the
things which he suffered.* (Heb. 5.7-8)

CHRISTIAN SCIENCE in English-speaking lands is the
most recent rival of the historic Christian faith. It bears so
manifestly the hall-mark of its founder, Mary Baker Eddy,
that it is impossible to understand it apart from the spiritual
odyssey of that lady.

She was born in 1821 in the New Hampshire town of Bow,
being the sixth child of a gentleman-farmer and his wife, who
were respected members of the Congregational Church. She
was a highly sensitive child who reacted strongly against the
stern and forbidding Calvinism of her father's creed. Her later
teaching was formulated in antagonism to the unchallenged
Calvinist tenet that trials and sorrows are natural and inevitable
and are sent by God for the spiritual strengthening of his
children. During most of her childhood she was subject to a
serious nervous illness which continued through many years of
adulthood. She was not only unfortunate in having an unsympathetic father, but also an unsympathetic husband. Her
first husband was a building-contractor, whose profits were
made by the exploitation of the slaves he owned. Soon after
the marriage, he died of yellow fever, leaving her with a small
son and considerable assets. These she employed in freeing the
slaves and in educating her child. The young widow then
married a dentist. So physically enfeebled was the bride that
Dr Patterson had to carry her downstairs from her room for

the ceremony and return her there on its completion. Patterson was also a scapegrace, who became infatuated with other women and left her to bring up her ailing child alone. However, he performed one good turn for his wife by introducing her to an unorthodox healer, renowned throughout New England as Phineas P. Quimby. He was a man of great personal magnetism. It was he who gave her many of the hints upon which she was to build up her system of Christian Science.[1] He claimed that there was only one cure for all diseases—the confidence of the patient in the healer.

He described his healing art in the following fashion: 'My practice,' he said, 'is unlike all medical practice. I give no medicine, and make no outward applications. I tell the patient his troubles, and what he thinks is his disease, and my explanation is the cure. If I succeed in correcting his errors, I change the fluids of the system, and establish the patient in health. The truth is the cure.'

Mrs Eddy's indebtedness to Quimby was greater than she cared to admit. His manuscripts, which have since been published, reveal that he referred to his new mind-healing system as 'Christian Science', and that he called disease 'an error', and this is, in fact, the most distinctive doctrine associated with the name of Mary Baker Eddy. 'Disease,' he wrote, 'is false reasoning. False reasoning is sickness and death.' On his death in 1866, Mrs Eddy did not merely repudiate her indebtedness to Quimby, but went so far as to claim that he had borrowed these ideas from her. Her conceited desire to claim absolute originality for her teaching resulted in the palpable untruth she wrote in her compendium of Christian Science:

> No human pen nor tongue taught me the science contained in the book.[2]

Mary Baker Patterson (as she was then named) presented herself in October 1862 at the International Hotel, Portland, Maine, to this Phineas P. Quimby. He told her that her animal spirit was reflecting its grief upon her body, and calling it spinal

---

[1] E. S. Bates and J. W. Dittemore, *The Truth and the Tradition* (Knopf, New York, 1932). See also Horatio Dresser, *The Quimby Manuscripts* (T. Y. Crowell, New York, 1921).

[2] *Science and Health* (authorized edn.), p. 110.

disease. He then dipped his hands in water, rubbed her head violently, and sent her into a mesmeric sleep. She awoke cured of her pain. The next day he repeated the treatment; the cure was as complete as it was swift. Moreover, there was no relapse. Her disease, she explained to Quimby, was cured by the healer's understanding of the truth of Christ brought by him into the world and lost for centuries, and not by Quimby's mesmerism. Quimby denied this, being an arrant unbeliever. But his patient refused to accept his disclaimer, and was so far restored to health that she mounted the hundred and eighty-two steps to the Dome of the City Hall to advertise to the world the greatness of Quimby.

She spent the next two years lecturing on Quimby and in trying to Christianize his faith-cures, by writing comments on his case-book. Meanwhile Quimby died of an ulcer in the stomach in 1866. This year is the date given for the official foundation of Christian Science. One can only conjecture that the reason was that now Quimby was dead, he could no longer dispute Mary Baker Patterson's claim to be the founder of Christian Science.

She began by treating private patients and by lecturing on the art of faith-healing. In 1875 there appeared her world-famous handbook *Science and Health*. Two years later she married Eddy, a business-man, the equable and congenial agent for a firm of sewing-machine manufacturers. Henceforward Christian Science was to stand upon a firm footing. Mr Asa Gilbert Eddy saw that the second and third editions of his wife's handbook were protected from literary piracy and thus safeguarded the copyright and the considerable profits. The new 'Bible' sold for three dollars a copy. Mr Eddy also introduced his wife to influential persons in Boston, where she lectured. He was her devoted missionary. After these days she never looked back. 3,284 churches and organizations acknowledge her as their spiritual leader. She founded a College, an organization with international ramifications, and a famous newspaper, *The Christian Science Monitor*.

She proved herself to be a woman of administrative ability, business acumen and dominating personality. Her logical and speculative abilities were of no mean order, and greatly outran her capacity for literary expression. Her greatest quality was her determination to help to heal the sorrows and ills of man-kind, for which she had a deep and lasting sympathy. She redis-covered and expressed in her own character the radiance that should be the distinguishing mark of the Christian life. This frail person was an astonishing example of the triumph of mind over matter until her death of pneumonia in 1910 at the age of eighty-nine. Christian Science now has an estimated world membership of 367,000.[1]

I

What was the key to her success and what were the benefits of her popular system? She undoubtedly gave a new sense of well-being to multitudes of neurotic and depressed persons. She radiated confidence and thousands of timid, melancholy and self-pitying people regained a sense of cheerful robustness and a faith to live by. It would be less than just to deny the two main values that her creed undoubtedly possessed: in a materialistic age she inculcated a belief in the spiritual inter-pretation of life, and she rediscovered the Christian art of faith-healing. Her system brought many other benefits also. She restored the notes of health and happiness to the Christian symphony. She also wisely taught her people to read both the Bible and *Science and Health* as a regular, daily discipline. It is undeniable that this method of meditation tends to produce calm and serene personalities. This taking time to be alone, to reflect and to pray, deserves imitation among orthodox Chris-tians. She effectively repudiated such unworthy notions of God as the belief that all pain is a divine imposition on God's chil-dren to teach them resignation. She propagated a profound belief in the goodness of God; so profound, in fact, that she met the age-old problem of evil in a divinely created universe by flatly denying its existence. She and her disciples were moti-vated by a deep sense of Christian charity. She deserves our gratitude for the happiness she has brought to thousands of

[1] See the basis on which this estimate is made in Charles S. Braden, *Christian Science Today* (Southern Methodist University Press, Dallas, Texas, 1958), p. 272. No official statistics are issued. In September 1962 there were 3,284 Christian Science churches and societies, as officially reported to A. Hoekema, *The Four Major Cults* (1963), p. 180. This was an increase of 818 from 1931.

mentally sick persons and for the stimulus she has been to the Christian Churches to return to psychological methods of healing.

I I

Her system of thought has been summarized by the author herself, as follows:

First, God is all in all.
Second, God is good. Good is mind.
Third, God, Spirit being all, nothing is matter.
Fourth, Life, God, omnipotent, good, deny death, evil, sin, disease—
Disease, sin, evil, death, deny good, omnipotent, God, Life.[1]

It will be immediately apparent that her system is based upon four categorical denials. She denies the existence of matter, pain, evil and death, all four of which historic Christianity is concerned to affirm as having a real existence in time. She declares, 'Material sense is nothing but a supposition of absence of Spirit.'[2] It is one thing to say that matter is not eternal; it is quite another to say that it does not exist at all. At the very outset this denial makes absurd the central Christian doctrine, that the Word of God became *flesh* and dwelt among us. Why was she prompted to make this denial contrary to all our human experience? Probably because she thought that the body was the source of all evil; but this is not so—for it is the imagination and the will that are the sources of sinfulness. For the Christian there is nothing evil in matter or in the world, except the misuse which we may make of either. Indeed, our spiritual worth is proven by the way we make use of our bodies.

In the second place, Mary Baker Eddy denies the existence of pain and sickness. Pain and suffering, she teaches, depend on our foolish belief in matter. She goes so far as to assert: 'A child may have worms, *if you say so,* or any other malady.'[3]

The boil simply manifests through inflammation and swelling a belief in pain, and this belief is called a boil.

[1] *Science and Health*, p. 113.   [2] *Ibid.*, p. 504.
[3] *Ibid.*, p. 413.

To this the only appropriate retort is to recite the limerick:

> There was a faith-healer of Deal,
> Who said, 'Although pain isn't real,
> When I sit on a pin
> And it punctures my skin,
> I dislike what I fancy I feel.'

It may readily be granted that pain is often exaggerated: nervous persons and hypochondriacs often imagine they are a prey to a disease which exists only in their fancies. Many people make themselves ill through sheer worrying. But it is totally different to assert that pain in all forms is sheer illusion. The heart of the Christian Gospel is that we have a suffering Saviour and that by faith in him we are able to transform suffering into blessing, sin into righteousness, death into eternal life. Our faith is built on that strange Man who hangs upon the Cross. It seems pertinent to ask: How can a faith be Christian, when it denies the reality of the Cross, the acknowledged centre and sign of historic Christianity? H. A. L. Fisher says, in the conclusion of *Our New Religion*:

> For the Christian Scientist a brilliant pioneer of drugless healing . . . replaces the suffering figure on the Cross.

Thirdly, Mrs Eddy denies the reality of evil and sin. She declares, 'Both sin and sickness are error, and Truth is their remedy.'[1] This denial issues from an honourable determination to 'justify the ways of God to man'. She preserves the unassailable goodness of God by the expedient of denying that sin and evil exist. To assert that sin does not exist, except as an illusion, is virtually to deny the saving work of Christ and to make his sufferings and death mere phantasms. Jesus, on the hypothesis of the Christian Scientists, laboured under the 'delusion' that sin was a reality. Either our Lord's desire to redeem mankind and obtain forgiveness for their sins was an error, or, at least, Jesus came only to prove that our belief in sin was mistaken. It is entirely characteristic of the escapism of Christian Science that it should publish so optimistic a journal as the famous *Christian Science Monitor*. It is understandable that it should

[1] *Ibid.*, p. 461.

not sensationalize crime or disaster, but this policy is carried out to the verge of blandness. There is little here to arouse indignation, alarm, or profound misgiving. By contrast, the realism of the Christian faith enables us to come to grips with the demonic power of evil by the example of Jesus Christ and in the power of the Holy Spirit.

In the fourth place, the existence of death is denied. Mrs Eddy asserts, 'Life is real and death is the illusion.'[1] Her reasoning seems to be that since we are essentially spiritual and the matter of our bodies is illusory, there is nothing left of us that can die. This, of course, is in open contradiction to the Christian faith which is born out of the Easter experience, when death was not evaded, but conquered by the risen Lord. Furthermore, this automatic immortality is at variance with the most solemn warnings of our Saviour and his apostles that there is a way of salvation and a way of damnation.

One is bound to admire the logical consistency of Mrs Eddy in her denials, but her life was not consistent with her declared beliefs. For example, she wore artificial teeth and spectacles, showing that her theories did not apply, at least, to diseases of the teeth and the eyes. A more serious inconsistency, however, was publicly revealed in a protest addressed to the trustees of Mrs Eddy by Mr John V. Dittemore (a former director of the Mother Church of Christian Science), in which he wrote:

> As you will know, Mrs Eddy employed physicians professionally, and took drugs on numerous occasions during the last ten years of her life.[2]

Her philosophy of life also falls under censure for serious misrepresentation of Christian doctrine in two important respects; namely, her teaching about the personality of God and of Jesus Christ. Her God is really impersonal, for

> Life, truth and love constitute the triune Person called God, that is, the triply Divine principle, Love.[3]

[1] *Ibid.*, p. 428.
[2] Reported in *The Christian World*, Feb. 28, 1929, and cited in Leslie D. Weatherhead, *Psychology in the Service of the Soul* (Epworth, 1949), p. 219.   [3] *Ibid.*, p. 331.

That she does not accept the Christian doctrine of the Holy Trinity appears from her avowal:

> Jesus demonstrated Christ; he proved that Christ is the divine idea of God—the Holy Ghost, or Comforter, revealing the divine Principle, Love.[1]

In fact, she invites us to believe in the impossible—an impersonal principle with personal attributes such as love.

Her account of Jesus Christ is equally unorthodox. She revives that most ancient of heresies, Docetism, in denying the reality of our Lord's human nature:

> Wearing in part a human form (that is, as it seemed to mortal view), being conceived by a human mother, Jesus was a Mediator between Spirit and the flesh, between Truth and error.[2]

She further denies that Jesus died by crucifixion. In her volume, *Miscellany*, she speaks of 'the supposedly crucified Christ', and interprets Romans 5.10 as meaning 'for when we were enemies, we were reconciled to God, by the seeming death of His Son'. Her claim to have surpassed the apostles in her understanding of the mission of Christ is contained in the following citation:

> Jesus' students, not sufficiently advanced fully to understand their Master's triumph, did not perform many wonderful works until they saw him after his crucifixion, and learned that he had not died.[3]

Clearly, if Christ did not die, neither could he be raised from the dead.

A denial of the reality of the Incarnation, the Cross and the Resurrection of Jesus Christ refutes entirely the claim that her system is a *Christian Science*.

III

Apart from these serious distortions and denials of the Christian message, Christian Science must be accounted

[1] *Science and Health*, p. 332.   [2] *Ibid.*, p. 315.
[3] *Ibid.*, p. 45.

dangerous for other reasons. Many lives have been lost through the inability of Mrs Baker Eddy to distinguish between illness caused by germ invasion and illness caused by psychological factors. H. A. L. Fisher avers in *Our New Religion* that the refusal of Christian Scientists to co-operate with members of the medical profession lays them open to the charge of being murderers. It is certain, at least, that they are parasites living upon the precautions of preventive medicine and public health. Furthermore, it is significant that although Christian Science has vast funds, opulent premises and enthusiastic workers, it is never found bringing its mission of health and happiness to the slums.

The Christian Scientists have little interest in either the social implications of the Gospel or even in mere sociability. They have no interest in lessening inter-ethnic tensions, in building orphanages or old-age homes for the poor, and their interest in higher education is restricted to founding institutions for the specific teaching of their own particular tenets. They do not even provide wholesome recreation for their own young people. This attitude, indeed, may be attributed to the view that evil is unreal and to recognize its existence institutionally would be to give it power.

Finally, Christian Science can fairly be accused of making religion a means to an end, for God is the means and the end is man's physical well-being. Like Spiritualism it must be accounted a 'Glory for me' and not a 'Glory for God' religion.

IV

These defects in the Christian Science system should make Christians all the more sensible of the greatness of the truth as it is in Christ Jesus. Its realism urges not an evasion of sin, suffering and death, but an attack upon them. A Christian is a follower of a Lord who said: 'In the world ye shall have tribulation, but be of good cheer, I have overcome the world.'

Further, the Gospel moves in a bracing, Christian Science in a relaxed, atmosphere. Jesus said, 'If any man will come after me, let him . . . take up his cross and follow me.' Mary Baker Eddy says, in effect, 'I invite you to a Christianity without tears.' But that cannot be! Christianity is only for those who offer the tears of repentance, who, like Peter, weep bitterly when they hear the cock crow, and remember their broken promises. It is a religion that speaks loudest in sighs, such as Mary's when she lamented, 'They have taken away my Lord and I know not where they have laid him.' Christianity offers a God who shall wipe away all tears. It is the divine answer to all our human sobbing—to the sobbing of the sinner, the sufferer and the bereft. If we are told that these experiences are unreal, we can only reply that the Christian Scientists are tone-deaf to the tragic notes of our human symphony. Life's foes demand to be faced with bracing realism, not evaded by Christian Science's escapism.

Christian Science is, in fact, a misnomer. It is neither Christian nor scientific. Mary Baker Eddy's cures are remembered, and rightly, with gratitude; her four casualties should not be forgotten—her three husbands and herself.

Further reading

Eddy, Mary Baker: her own writings are the basic sources for the study of Christian Science and the chief of them, all published by the Christian Science Publishing Society, Boston, Mass., are: *Science and Health, with Key to the Scriptures* and *Miscellaneous Writings*

Fisher, H. A. L., *Our New Religion* (Watts, London, 1929)

Braden, C. S., *Christian Science Today* (Southern Methodist University Press, Dallas, 1958)

Powell, Lyman P., *Mary Baker Eddy* (L. P. Powell, New York, 1930)

Ramsey, E. M., *Christian Science and its Discoverer* (Boston, Mass., 1935)

Swihart, Altman K., *Since Mrs Eddy* (Henry Holt and Co., New York, 1931) is an account of two movements of deviation from Christian Science

Wilbur, Sibyl, *The Life of Mary Baker Eddy* (Christian Science Publishing Co., Boston, Mass., 1938), the official life

9

SPIRITISM

Try the spirits whether they be of God.   (I John 4.1)

I

SPIRITISM, the belief that the spirits of the departed actually communicate with the living, is often erroneously styled *Spiritualism*, but Christians repudiate this claim to spirituality on the part of a cult which uses material proofs. How can the attraction[1] that Spiritism has for its devotees be accounted for? It is suggested that three factors explain its contemporary allurement.

The first and most important factor is the deep longing of the bereaved human heart to know whether its beloved dead survive in another world. It is the men and women who sigh, 'O for the touch of a vanished hand and the sound of a voice that is still', who go to spiritistic seances. It is no cause for wonderment that Spiritism should flourish in an age which has seen two major world wars in three decades. For the attitude of distracted persons twice bereaved in a life-time one can have no scorn, but only a profound sympathy.

The second reason for the success of this cult is that three figures of national importance in Great Britain were avowed Spiritists; namely, Sir Arthur Conan Doyle (distinguished novelist and creator of 'Sherlock Holmes', the father of an impressive progeny of literary detectives), Sir Oliver Lodge and

[1] According to *The Sunday Times* (issue of July 24, 1960) there are about 1,000 Spiritualist churches with a membership of 250,000 in Britain. In the U.S.A. the five Spiritualist associations have a total membership of 178,855 (*Yearbook of the American Churches for 1964*, published by the National Council of the Churches of Christ in America, New York).

Sir William Crookes, the eminent scientists. Spiritism's most renowned contemporary champion is Lord Dowding, former Chief of the Royal Air Force. These men gave to Spiritism the appearance of being a trustworthy creed because they subscribed to it. At the same time, it should not be forgotten that Sir Oliver Lodge condemned much Spiritism as quackery and superstition. It should also be remembered that a man who is an expert in the physical sciences is not thereby automatically qualified as an expert in the spiritual world.

Success has come to Spiritism for a third reason; because many people are under the impression that it is a form of Christianity, owning an allegiance to Jesus Christ. Such confusion was to be expected (possibly was actually encouraged) when the Spiritist assemblies met in buildings with such names as 'The Church of Christian Fellowship', 'The Temple of the Holy Trinity', or 'The Church of the Spirit'. Despite some similarities in teaching, however, it will be seen that there are wide differences between Christianity and Spiritism.

Though this cult has a modern flavour, it has an ancient lineage. In one sense it might be described as a refined form of ancestor worship. It can be traced back to the most primitive form of religion—animism, which attributed souls or spirits to trees, streams and stones. In the dawn of civilization it was customary to explain the eerie and unaccountable phenomena by reference to the visitation of the spirits of the dead. It was fear-engirded and only a man as desperate as Saul resorted to the witch of Endor to conjure up the dead. The subject was regarded with awesome dread: it was thought to be dangerous and even demonic. The practice was forbidden in the Old Testament and declared to be against the will of God.

Modern Spiritism originated in 1847 in Hydeville in the State of New York, with the announcement that strange revelations through mysterious noises and rappings had been made to Margaret and Kate Fox, children of twelve and nine years, respectively. The children claimed that the spirits sent them messages in answer to their questions in a type of code. Three raps were interpreted as an affirmative answer, one rap as a negative, and two raps as doubtful. The children were pronounced to be 'mediums' and from widespread interest in their supposed achievements arose the multiplication of arranged sittings or seances which are the recognized methods of organizing Spiritist meetings today. As a result many mediums took up the occult as a lucrative profession and brought the subject into disrepute. A more important result, however, was the foundation of an important body of sincere scientific investigators in 1882, *The Society for Psychical Research*. The proceedings of this society constitute a most impressive examination of all Spiritist claims. They have established the existence of some remarkable phenomena, but the interpretation of these experiences is inconclusive.

II

In justice to Spiritism it must be acknowledged that its teaching and Christianity have a considerable area of common ground. Both agree that man is not simply a complicated body; both hold, in fact, that man is a soul and a body. Moreover, both parties are agreed that individuality survives the disintegration of the body and continues to exercise its faculties. Also, both agree that the resurrection of Jesus Christ is a reality of profound significance.

Furthermore, Spiritists have emphasized that love is the sole and triumphant operative power in the universe, a belief which is closely akin to the Christian claim that God is holy love. In addition, there is a close affinity between the teaching of Spiritism and the article of the Apostles' Creed which Christians profess: 'I believe in the Communion of Saints.' In face of contemporary materialism, atheism and agnosticism the importance of these common tenets is considerable and to this extent Spiritism and Christianity can be regarded as allies.

The likeness between certain fundamental Christian and Spiritualist tenets can be discerned from the following *Declaration of Principles* issued by the National Spiritualist Association, which was founded in Chicago in 1893. It reads:

1. We believe in Infinite Intelligence.
2. We believe that the phenomena of Nature, both physical and spiritual, are the expression of Infinite Intelligence.
3. We affirm that a correct understanding of such expression and living in accordance therewith constitute true religion.

4. We affirm that the existence and personal identity of the individual continue after the change called death.
5. We affirm that communication with the so-called dead is a fact scientifically proven by the phenomena of Spiritualism.
6. We believe that the highest morality is contained in the Golden Rule. . . .
7. We affirm the moral responsibility of the individual, and that he makes his own happiness or unhappiness as he obeys or disobeys Nature's physical or spiritual laws.
8. We affirm that the doorway to reformation is never closed against any human soul, here or hereafter.[1]

Nonetheless, there are areas of complete divergence between historic Christianity and Spiritualism which must now be considered.

III

What, then, are these differences and are they important? In general, the differences are both in the manner the information is obtained and in the character and quality of that information.

Christianity believes that man is both spiritual and physical. The doctrine is derived by Christians partly from philosophy but mainly from the life and teaching of Jesus Christ. Christianity's belief in a future life is founded upon God's mighty act in raising Jesus Christ from the grave and upon our Lord's promise, 'If I live, ye shall live also.'

The Spiritists claim that their information on survival after death and the nature of the after-life is received from the dead themselves; that is, from controls who are supposed to transmit their messages through a medium in a trance in the darkness. This claim, however, cannot admit of proof by its very nature. The dilemma has been admirably stated by Dr Glenn Atkins thus:

On the one hand, only those things which are utterly *unknown* to the living anywhere can be finally and conclusively a testimony to communications from the dead. On the other hand, unless the information thus received is *known*

[1] Frank S. Mead, *Handbook of Denominations in the United States* (revised edn., Abingdon Press, New York and Nashville, 1956), p. 198.

to the living, its truth or falsity can never be proved or dis-
proved.[1]

Furthermore, the mediums who claim to be in touch with the
spirits 'on the other side' are not conspicuously intelligent. Even
Sir Oliver Lodge reluctantly describes them as generally 'not
particularly able or highly educated folk'. Dr James Black
evinces a Christian's bewilderment at this fact, as follows:

> With the best will in the world, I cannot understand why
> spirits, presumably purified from the clogging influences of
> the body, should choose to manifest themselves only or
> mainly to people of this order. If they manifested them-
> selves to saintly souls or to those who live on a high spiritual
> and mental level, I could at once appreciate this. . . .
> Frankly I am puzzled and disturbed by it. God has always
> chosen the finest instruments to proclaim his finest message.[2]

By contrast, our information as Christians is received
through faith in a Master of Life, whose words we can challenge, and whose character and teaching force us to admit by
their quality that they are a revelation of God's very nature.
The information of Spiritists is obtained from a stranger of
whom they know nothing, through the offices of a medium
about whom they know next to nothing.

The second divergence between Spiritism and Christianity
is seen in the nature of that future life which both systems
depict. Spiritists, moreover, claim that the future life is the
prerogative of man, simply as man. The Christian, however,
claims that God alone is immortal and that he confers the
privilege of eternal life with him only on those who have tried
to do his will. Spiritists believe in an automatic future life:
Christians believe in eternal life that God alone can give out of
his grace. For this eternal life the individual must fulfil certain
moral and spiritual conditions. Christians find it hard to believe that every blackguard after his life is over finds immediate
entry into God's holy presence. Nor do they believe that God
can be uninterested in the difference between right and wrong.

---

[1] *Modern Religious Cults and Movements* (Allen and Unwin,
1923), p. 313.
[2] *New Forms of the Old Faith*, pp. 90-1.

Such a conception is impossibly sentimental for them because they believe that the Judge of all the earth is just.

Furthermore, as will be seen later, the Spiritist's picture of life after death is spiritually superficial and tawdry, compared with the richly meaningful Christian conception of eternity. Christians must repudiate any conception of the after-life which regards it essentially as an automatic rest-cure and not primarily as the blessedness of everlasting fellowship with God and his saints. These are real differences and we injure our holy faith if we attempt to gloss them over.

IV

The Christian criticism of Spiritism makes eight serious charges against it, now to be detailed. The first accusation is that Spiritism is frequently a selfish philosophy of life. It encourages adherents to join its ranks for what they can get out of it. In Bede Frost's pointed epigram, it is a 'glory for me, not a glory for God religion'. It tries to satisfy the personal craving for certainty in spiritual things. It also appeals to the natural man's desire for a heavenly superannuation on easy terms. It is too comfortable a religion: it is, in short, Christianity without the Cross. It does not encourage service for others, nor does it issue a challenge to rebuild the world after God's heart. It appeals not to the heroic motives, but to man's desire for security. For our Lord's advice, 'He that loseth his life shall save it', it substitutes the tame motto of 'Safety First'.

The superiority of the Christian faith is seen in the fact that Jesus appeals to both motives. He who said, 'Come unto me all ye that labour and are heavy-laden, and I will give you rest', also said, 'He that would come after me, let him take up his cross and follow me.' It is true that he promised that his followers should reign with him in everlasting life, but St Paul is true to his Master in declaring, 'Those who suffer with him shall also reign with him.' Spiritism offers security, but at too cheap a price. Victory is promised, but without the triumph of a successful struggle. Those who are not spiritual invalids and those who are dissatisfied with the world as it is and wish to remould it, prefer the invigoration of fighting behind the Cross of Christ.

Despite its preferred name of 'Spiritualism', Spiritism is often a materialistic religion. This is Christianity's second censure against it. What is so disappointing about Spiritism is the utterly terrestrial nature of the heaven it offers. Heaven is pictured in purely physical terms; it is imagined as a celestial garden city with all the modern conveniences. Should the reader think that this is a gross exaggeration, let him mark the following words which are a record of what the control, Pheneas, is supposed to have told Lady Conan Doyle:

> Your home in the other world is ready for you. There is a round small building in the grounds which is filled with exquisite coloured vibrations into which you go when you want your soul's rejuvenation. . . . There is an oblong pond round which coloured birds come to drink.

'Coloured vibrations', the reader will note, are bodily sensations—pleasant to the eye and tingling to the spine. But what have such sensory impressions to do with the soul?

Revelations received from other mediums only confirm the impression that this heaven of the Spiritists is the projection of tired spirits in search of a spa and a pump-room. The following excerpt, extracted from the Handbook to Heaven entitled *Spirit Intercourse*, is sufficient evidence for the charge:

> Summer land is 1,350 miles from the earth; light, 100-110 degrees. Pet animals and birds numerous. Flowers and fruit in rich abundance; habitations of brick and stone interspersed with gardens.

The other advantages are left to our imagination to depict. In the same vein the catalogue might be continued to include comfortably furnished apartments, with electricity, hot and cold water, and all the usual conveniences. If that is heaven, one can as easily imagine a sprightly St Peter as receptionist, walking down a spiral staircase in spats, wearing immaculate morning-dress, with a carnation in his button-hole and a watch-chain on which hangs a bunch of golden keys! This uncelestial cavalcade will not do for Christians. Men and women could be gulled by such a materialist picture of heaven only because they have never understood the meaning of eternal life as it is declared by Christ. Otherwise, they would have rejected so spurious an imitation. The Spiritist afterlife is too like Valhalla or the Paradise of fleshly Moslem expectation.

The third charge against Spiritism is that its revelation is untheological—it tells us nothing about God. It seems that communion with God is nowhere envisaged. In fact, God seems to the Spiritists to be entirely uninterested in man, and man's interest in God is purely speculative. Is it too much to say with Dr James Black 'the one thing that Spiritualism lacks is the "spiritual"'?[1] The paucity of references to God in the communications of the controls might lead one to believe that God is entirely an afterthought, instead of being the only conceivable ground and guarantee of the survival of the soul beyond death.

The fourth charge against Spiritism is that it can be a dangerous faith. It is not denied that spirits might have intercourse with human beings. The Bible, in fact, clearly asserts that there are two kinds of spirits—good and evil. Believers are warned, 'Try the spirits, whether they be of God.' And, in this connexion, Spiritists themselves admit not only that frauds have taken place in seances, but that evil spirits are occasionally present. The following warning is taken from a book written by a psychic medium, who herself exercised a spiritist practice for over twenty years. The book is *Voices from the Void* and its author is Mrs Travers Smith (or Hesther Dowden, her maiden name).

If I may venture to advise persons who long to speak once more with persons who have vanished into darkness, I should say it is wise and sane not to make the attempt. The chances against genuine communication are about ten to one: the disappointments and doubts connected with the experiments are great.

Her *caveat* was repeated in a book she published in 1920. There can be no doubt that occult trafficking is dangerous for anxious, excitable and neurotic people, and such investigation should be left in the hands of the accredited societies engaged in psychic experiments. Spiritism is not only dangerous to sanity, it is also a menace to faith. L. W. Grensted offered this wise advice:

[1] *Ibid.*, p. 103.

The traffic in signs, the miracle-mongering not for the sake of love but for the sake of the miracle, the quest for manifestations and the rest, can become a most perilous distraction, separating the Spirit alike from God and from the everyday world in which God's work must be done.[1]

At heart Spiritism is not trust in God; it is born of distrust of him. It is an attempt to substitute experimental certainty for faith. It is the monstrous design to subject God to the indignity of a test-tube examination. It should be repudiated, as our Lord repudiated the Evil One: 'Thou shalt not tempt the Lord thy God.'

Our Saviour continually warned his disciples against those who wanted 'signs' or positive demonstrations and who refused to take anything on trust. 'This wicked and adulterous generation seeketh a sign, but it shall not be given unto it.' Our Lord showed in the parable of Dives and Lazarus that no messages from the dead can supplant or confirm a living faith. Jesus depicts the rich man asking that a messenger be sent to his brothers on earth to warn them about the reality of the future life. But the answer was given, 'They have Moses and the prophets; let them hear them. . . . If they hear not Moses and the prophets, neither will they be persuaded, though one rose from the dead.' St Paul plainly re-issued the warning when he counselled Timothy: 'But the Spirit plainly saith that in after times some will fall away from the faith, giving heed to deceiving spirits, and teaching of demons, through the impostures of these who speak falsely, men seared in their own consciences.'

Spiritism's success should be a warning to all faithful Christians that when the Christian faith in God and knowledge of God is diluted, vapid and vague, then pale imitations of the original find a ready market amongst the credulous.

The sixth count against Spiritism is that its claims are inconclusive. While it may be admitted that the Spiritists present us with phenomena which transcend our normal experience, it cannot be accepted that the only explanation for these is the agency of departed spirits. At least four explanations have been offered to account for these phenomena. Some have attributed them to fraud. Others have said that they are self-deception—

[1] *Expository Times*, Vol. LIV, p. 203.

the unintended giving away of personal information to the medium or a temporary lapse in concentration of observation on the part of the person attending a seance. Others, again, have attributed it to a collective unconsciousness into which the medium delves. A most promising alternative explanation connects the phenomena with telepathy—the communication of thoughts from one mind to another bypassing the usual five senses. Roman Catholics, for their part, urge that all the spirits taking part in the seances are evil spirits. Amid this variety of explanations, the only verdict on the Spiritist claims must be that of 'Not proven'.

The seventh charge against Spiritism is that it is unnecessary. A spiritual faith is in no need of physical attestation. Belief in the future life after death of human souls does not rest on miraculous testimony but on our faith in the character and fidelity and promises of the God and Father of the Risen Christ. Spiritism is therefore otiose.

The eighth and final charge against Spiritism is that it contains elements of the suspicious and the ridiculous. Seance rooms hold their proceedings in darkness, preventing any possibility of seeing and examining the evidence; there is an entire absence of normal control; and even the 'temperamental' nature of some mediums is bound to lend suspicion to seances. G. K. Chesterton has satirized the element of the ridiculous in his sceptical question: 'Do you expect to hear the voice of God calling from a coal-cellar?' The answer is that God's voice is heard saying of Jesus, 'This is my beloved Son: hear ye him.' And that beloved Son has said simply, 'In my Father's house are many mansions. I go to prepare a place for you. If it were not so, I would have told you.' Trusting him, the first-born from the dead, we take his promise on trust. Experiments are unnecessary where faith prevails.

> I know not where his islands lift
>   Their fronded palms in air;
> I only know I cannot drift
>   Beyond his love and care.

That is all we know and all we need to know. A spiritual faith cannot rest on materialistic proofs. The sole foundation for our belief in eternity as Christians must be God's promise and 'the exceeding greatness of his power to usward who believe, according to the working of the strength of his might, which he wrought in Christ when he raised him from the dead'.

Further reading

The Spiritualist Manual (National Spiritualist Association, Washington, D.C., 7th edn., 1944)

Lawton, George S., *The Drama of Life after Death* (Henry Holt and Co., New York, 1932)

Wright, J. Stafford, *What is Man?* (Paternoster Press, London, 1954)

West, D. J., *Psychical Research Today* (Penguin Books, London, 1962)

10

THEOSOPHY

Beware of anyone getting hold of you by means of a theosophy which is specious make-believe, on the lines of human tradition, corresponding to the elemental spirits of the world and not to Christ.

(Col. 2.8)

PART of the attraction of Theosophy is to be found in its impressive title. Originally the name meant no more than 'a knowledge of things Divine', a designation which each other religion might claim for its own. In time, however, it came to carry overtones of meaning, implying that this was a superior and unusually intimate knowledge of God, reserved only for the intellectually and spiritually advanced. It further suggested that this esoteric system of doctrines and rites was occult and reserved only for the initiated. Its first appeal, therefore, is clearly to the pride of the select intellect.

The other attractions of Theosophy are, it seems, to defend the justice of the moral order, to offer a prospect of spiritual progress here and hereafter, and its profession to deliver its devotees from all constricting theological or ecclesiastical loyalties.

The renewal of interest in Theosophy is also related to the contemporary interest in Buddhism among intellectuals and 'beatniks'. Its gentle scepticism and deep compassion for all creatures, as well as its inspiration of some *outré* forms of art, all contribute to make it attractive to those who seek the unusual and the esoteric.

Although it originates from the time of the mystery religions and the Gnostics, its contemporary form has a modern derivation. It commenced when the Theosophical Society was founded by Madame Blavatsky and Colonel Olcott in New York in 1875. The Society was intended to compare the methods of Spiritualism with those of the old Jewish and Egyptian Cabbalas. America proving too pragmatic and deficient in the appreciation of mysticism, Madame Blavatsky went to India in 1878 where she gained an immediate and widespread success. She gathered a group of enthusiastic Indian and European disciples around her and together they studied the speculations of the Eastern mystics. She claimed to be in touch with the Great White Brotherhood of Tibet who were, in her own words, a 'Lodge of Masters or Adepts' in the spiritual life. The Society for Psychical Research investigated this claim but pronounced it fraudulent. After this exposure in 1885, she left Madras. In the ensuing six years of her life, she produced her book, *Secret Doctrine*, which is the catechism of modern Theosophy. This body of teaching was later systematized and developed by Mrs Annie Besant, who gained a respectful hearing for Theosophy among intelligent and cultured people. G. K. Chesterton's recipe for Theosophy aptly summarizes its origin: Asia and Evolution and the English lady; and I think they would be better apart.'

It is important to notice that the cult originated in India. The Easterner and the Westerner look through the world with different eyes. The man of the East is naturally a mystic: he is more interested in the inner world of meditation than in the outward world of phenomena and investigation. His religion is apt to be an escape from the world to God. Indeed, he claims to find God by premature retirement from the world.

By contrast, the religion of the man of the West is more a desire to remould the world according to the Divine plan. Edward Vernon declares that the symbol of the East is the temple, while the symbol of the West is the scientific laboratory. The East looks inward, the West outward. Or, in psychological terms, the man of the East is an introvert, while the man of the West is an extrovert. Perhaps, however, the best distinction drawn between East and West in religion is Chesterton's. 'The Buddhist saint,' he said, 'has his eyes shut, whilst the Christian saint has his eyes open.' Theosophy, although it claims to be the universal religion, is very much the product of the East, living in the atmosphere of introspection, asceticism and withdrawal from the world, which characterizes the religions of the East.

The Theosophical Society today considers itself 'an absolutely unsectarian body of seekers after Truth, striving to serve humanity and revive the religious spirit'. It has three declared aims: '(1) To form a nucleus of the Universal Brotherhood of Humanity, without distinction of race, creed, sex, caste or colour. (2) To encourage the study of Comparative Religion, Philosophy and Science. (3) To investigate unexplained laws of Nature and the powers latent in man.'

I

The claims of Theosophy must now be considered, especially its implicit belief in karma and reincarnation. As previously indicated, its chief claim is to be the universal religion. Had it not borrowed its doctrines almost exclusively from the East, the claim might have some truth in it. In fact, however, the idea of the unknowability of God derives from the Hindu *Upanishads*, the ideal of detachment from an illusory world is borrowed from Buddhism, as also the doctrine of successive human reincarnations. Furthermore, its methods of attaining to religious peace are all of Eastern origin.

Its claim to be the universal religion cannot be accepted for two other reasons. One is that a religion for spiritual experts only is bound to appeal to a minority, never to the majority, as a universal religion must do. But the most compelling reason against the belief that it is the universal religion is that syncretism takes place only at the cost of destroying all that is distinctive in differing religions. Christianity and Buddhism, for example, will not mix. The Christian ideal of the future life is the perfection of the self, the Buddhist the annihilation of all selfhood.

The second major claim of Theosophy is to be a compound of modern science and ancient philosophy. This is rapidly disposed of by Dr James Black, as he argues that

The Eastern speculation of reincarnation, i.e. souls after death being reborn into another human life, is totally against the proved findings of the science of heredity, where off-springs are known to inherit not only their physical life, but also their powers and capabilities from their parents and ancestry.[1]

II

The doctrines of Theosophy can be viewed from three vantage-points.

Their teaching about God. Theosophists are Pantheists. In their own words: 'All that is is God, and God is all that is.' This insistence upon the unity of God seems to be admirable, until it is examined. When pushed to its logical conclusion, however, its absurdity is patent. If God is everything and everything is God, then God is as much in an archangel as in an atom-bomb, as much in the sunset as in the seaweed, as much in a cherub as in a crocodile, as much in ameliorative medicine as in a microbe, and as much in a martyr as in a mosquito.

But, the Theosophist hastens to explain, all these things were created by God and God wills them to exist. It is true that they are the materials for our human struggle, the fulcrum for our spiritual leverage; but it is idle to pretend that God is indifferent as to whether the microbe slays the man, or the man slays the microbe. Then the Theosophist replies scathingly, 'But you are mistaken. It is foolish to describe God as personal. Would you endow God with the limitations of a finite human personality? He is neither interested nor disinterested, because God is not a he at all. He is suprapersonal.'

It is here that the argument breaks off, because the term 'God' is interpreted differently by the Christian and the Theosophist. What the Christian regards as the noblest way of defining God, the Theosophist takes as an insult to his Deity. If both Christian and Theosophist regard the world as a prison-house, there the agreement ends. The Theosophist is eagerly searching for a key with which to escape. The Christian, on the other hand, is thinking of the other poor spirits confined in the same prison. He is eager to transform convicts into reformed characters. The Christian's greatest stimulus to reformation is the belief that Christ demands that he love his

[1] *New Forms of the Old Faith* (Nelson, 1948), p. 58.

neighbour as himself. He is the brother for whom Christ died. For the Christian, therefore, the world is neither good nor bad; it is neutral. It is the school of character, 'the vale of soul-making', the edge which sharpens the soul into an instrument to improve the world. The Theosophist says, 'I accept', or 'I resign'. The Christian says, 'I resist'.

The fundamental difference in outlook is due to a basic difference in the conception of God. The Theosophist's God is impersonal Justice. The Christian's God co-operates with man to make all things work together for good.

In addition, Theosophy falls under censure for its inherent contradiction. For, while it urges that God is impersonal, the 'Super-consciousness', the Deity is given such personal attributes as 'loving', 'just', and 'truthful'.

Furthermore, the Christology of the Theosophists is seriously defective and arbitrarily unhistorical. Mrs Besant has had the effrontery to produce her own Gospel. According to her, Jesus was born a hundred years before his presumed nativity, was trained in a desert community of the Essenes, where he learned the esoteric wisdom of the East from visiting Indian and Egyptian sages. She further maintains that the 'Christ' part of his nature was added at Baptism but withdrawn during the Crucifixion and that he returned to teach his disciples the mysteries for a period of fifty years. She equates Jesus with Buddha and Confucius as one of the Masters of the spiritual life. Christian orthodoxy cannot accept this caricature of the Founder of the Faith.

The Theosophist teaching about man and salvation. The Theosophists have a peculiar doctrine of man. They assert that each individual is compounded of seven parts. The most common classification is the following: the physical body, the etheric double (or vital body), the astral (or emotional) body, the mental body, the causal body, the future body, the perfected body. Salvation consists in moving from body to body until perfection is reached in the seventh body. Successively, the unimportant parts of the self are sloughed off like the unwanted skins of a snake. Or, in the biting words of Father Bede Frost, this is 'the strip-tease of the soul'.

What is to be thought of this teaching concerning the seven parts or bodies of man? To say the least of it, it is very muddled psychology. Man cannot be divided into physical, vital, emotional, mental and volitional parts and retain the unity of his personality. All these faculties of man are employed simultaneously, not successively. A simple instance may be taken—that of a footballer scoring a goal. The kick is physical, the placing of the kick is mental, the fact that the toe connects with the ball is vital, the will to kick is volitional, and the joy that a good kick brings is emotional; these are all parts of one simultaneous reaction and action. They are only divisible on reflection, not in action. Indeed, if they took place successively, it is doubtful if any footballer would ever score a goal! Human personality cannot be divided into five parts, let alone seven. As for the future body or the perfect body, there seems to be no relation between them and the present personality of man. This psychology is confused because it isolates parts of human life that co-exist and refuse to be parted in the actual texture of experience.

But an even more serious criticism must be offered of the salvation envisaged by the Theosophists. It consists in killing the body that the soul may live. But the body is not evil, it is the instrument of the soul. It is the medium through which the soul communicates with the outer world and with other souls. What alone is evil is the abuse of the body.

Theosophists make the mistake of saying, 'Get rid of the body and you get rid of evil.' But, as Jesus reminded his disciples, it is evil thoughts that corrupt, not the body. Salvation must be wrought in the inner citadel of the mind and imagination; therefore there is no real salvation to be found in mortifying the body, which is only the agent of evil thoughts and imaginings. Evil is not like a stain on the polished table that soils the surface; it is far more akin to dry rot that weakens and then destroys the interior of the wood. Humanity needs a new inner constitution, but the Theosophists offer us only French polishing. Our need is not evolution, but revolution.

The teaching about reincarnation. This is the most distinctive and important Theosophical tenet. It is this aspect of Theosophy which has attracted several men of distinction in the Western world, including Aldous Huxley and J. B. Priestley. In fact, the fine series of 'Time-plays' written by Priestley have this as their central theme.

Like Christians, Theosophists have to unravel the age-old problem of the suffering of the innocent. How can they reconcile this with the belief in a wise and benevolent God? The Christian admits the difficulty. His tentative answer is that since we are bound together as families and nations the innocent must suffer with the guilty, for that is the price to be paid for human fellowship. Moreover, since God suffers in the afflictions of his people this tragic experience can be transmuted to gain where it is accepted in faith, for suffering then becomes an impetus to Christian love.

Theosophy takes an easier path. It denies that there is any problem, since it denies that there are any innocent persons. We are all supposed to be suffering for sins committed in previous existences or reaping the advantages of previous virtues. We therefore deserve the penalties or rewards dealt out to us in this life. Thus if we are born diseased or defective, or in the midst of crime or poverty, it is the recompense of our former evil deeds; if we have noble dispositions, great abilities, or high positions, these were won by our own former merits. This is undeniably an attractive belief because it reconciles the suffering in the world with the justice of God.

Its fundamental weakness lies in its failure to explain how suffering does benefit us. If I was a murderer in my last life and I am born deformed in this life, it is a judgment that I deserve. But, since I cannot recall the circumstances under which I was prompted to commit murder, how can such a judgment teach me repentance? How can I repent sins whose origin and nature I have forgotten? Since I cannot feel sorry, how can I improve? Moreover, if I am born deformed, I have no information to assure me that it was a just punishment. Is there more reason why I should say, 'I deserve it', than that I should curse the universe for my misfortune? These are some of the obstinate questions the doctrine of reincarnation provokes in Christian minds.

Furthermore, Theosophy, while professing to explain the inequalities of life, succeeds only in making them disappear in the mists of the past. We are then forced to ask, What caused the first unequal conditions or the first unequal actions?

Possibly the worst feature of the doctrine of reincarnation is that it paralyses the desire to improve the social environment and produces an ignoble fatalism. Since action is the fruit of desire, and desire must be abandoned, action is prohibited.

Moreover, it is no palliation to be told that things will be better in another existence. We wish to make the best of this life here and now. This belief in an impersonal justice has no dynamic in it. It is a conservatism of the soul, a religion of long-deferred hope.

Even the future life posited by Theosophy is only a pale shadow of the Christian doctrine of eternal life, not only because its realization may be almost indefinitely postponed, but also because it offers absorption or annihilation of individuality in the Infinite as its goal. The Christian doctrine of the perfection of the self is its complete contrary.

III

The chief criticism of Theosophy is that it appeals to the self-regarding motives. Its advice is, 'Make it easier for yourself in the next life.' This plea must be rejected by the Christian because he is not concerned primarily for a more comfortable existence in another world for himself; he wants a finer existence for his brethren in this world. He desires to be a reformer, not a pensioner. He cannot worship a God who is impartial justice. How can the thought of a Divine pair of scales either inspire or comfort him? He needs a God who bleeds with humanity in its wounds and scars. He wants a God who will redeem society and remake man in his own image. He requires a saviour and a friend. He therefore turns to God's eternal and beloved Son, the carpenter of Nazareth, whose hands are blunted in life's workshop, the loving Teacher and Companion of the common people. He turns to the lonely crucified Son of God on the stark hill-top, who took his station among thieves.

The God of the Theosophists is too highbrow for the Christian. Their God is no more interested in our human struggle than a sleeping and gigantic elephant. The God of the Theosophists is busied with his mathematical calculations, apportioning exact retribution to our sins in different existences. His Impersonal Highness is, in short, merely a celestial calculating-machine.

Christians cannot be persuaded to leave the God who met them in Christ Jesus and, without any assurance save their need, embraced them in the arms outspread on the jagged tree of Calvary. They stake their life on the fact that this God cares, because he treats our erring humanity so patiently; because, also, 'he gave his only-begotten Son that whosoever believeth on him should not perish but have everlasting life'. Christ is the proof that God cares. In him God gave us his Word.

IV

The grandeur of the Christian faith is seen in comparison with the deficiencies in Theosophy which it can supply. Christianity offers us a true view of sin. For the Theosophist a sense of personal sin is thought of as weak and degrading. Forgiveness, too, is inadmissible for the Theosophist because it would represent a diminution of strict justice. No new start is possible for the Theosophist in this life, but only in the next, and a man must work out his own slow salvation without the assistance of God.

There is no redemption from the power of evil in Theosophy, either. The World Teachers or Bodhisattvas of Theosophy offer teaching and enlightenment and, occasionally, example. But human nature needs more—it requires the infusion of new life. It is only Jesus Christ who said, 'I am come that they might have life and have it more abundantly.'

Theosophy knows little of the meaning of sacrifice, which includes vicarious suffering. Their ideal man practises detachment to kill desire. But this is a striking contrast to the Saviour, who 'though he was a Son, yet learned obedience through the things which he suffered', who 'was in all points tempted like as we are, yet without sin', who, as the Sinless Penitent, 'hath borne our griefs and carried our sorrows'.

Because of Christ's coming to serve the world, Christians cannot be content with their own salvation. They can rest only when the kingdoms of this world have become kingdoms of our God and of his Christ. There is only one faith to live by: the faith of the Apostles, enshrined in the Creed of that name. This has been admirably summed up by Dr Norman Macleod thus: 'There is a Father in Heaven who loves us, a Brother who died for us, and a Spirit who helps us to be good, and a Home where we shall all meet at the last.' That is a creed that will see humanity through this life into the next. It is, if need be, a creed to die for; it is assuredly a creed to live for.

Further reading

The chief original sources of the cult are Helena Blavatsky's *Isis Unveiled* and *The Secret Doctrine*. The writings of Annie Besant and Charles W. Leadbeater are also important, especially the latter's *Outline to Theosophy* and *Textbook of Theosophy*

Farquhar, J. N., *Modern Religious Movements in India* (Macmillan, London and New York, 1918)

Kuhn, Alvin B., *Theosophy, a Modern Revival of Ancient Wisdom* (Henry Holt and Co., New York, 1930)

Ransome, Josephine, *A Short History of the Theosophic Society* (Theosophical Publishing House, Adyar, India, 1938)

11

A SURVEY

*Jesus said, 'I am the way, the truth, and the life; no
one cometh unto the Father, but by me.'* (John 14.6)

FROM the first day of the Christian Church, Christians have
had to fight the battle of faith on two fronts: spiritual and
intellectual. While the martyrs outlived and outdied their
opponents, the apologists out-thought them.

The task of apologetics, the intellectual defence of the
Christian faith, changes from age to age, as new opponents
arise to challenge Christian doctrine. None the less, throughout
church history the systems that rival Christianity appear to fall
into four main classes: (1) the denial of spiritual values and of
the existence of God, which may be termed atheism on its
intellectual side, and materialism or secularism on its cultural
and social side; (2) the claims to finality made by religions
other than Christianity; (3) a Judaistic perversion of the Christian faith; (4) a Gnostic eclecticism, and anthology of Christian
and non-Christian beliefs. Our concern is exclusively with the
perversions and distortions of Christianity such as are included
within the third and fourth categories.

I

The first council of the Christian Church in Jerusalem had
to face the living issue: how much Judaism shall non-Jewish
converts to the Christian faith be expected to embrace? Was
the Law valid now that Christians lived under the sphere of
grace? Judaistic Christianity has sometimes been described as
the retention of the scaffolding even when the headstone of the

corner has been placed in position: that is, an attempt to gain salvation by obedience to the prescriptions of the Jewish Law, instead of a life of trust in the merits and mediation of Jesus Christ in the strength of the Holy Spirit. Many Christians in all centuries have found it difficult to accept the ethical imperative of love. They would prefer to regard their religion as the observance of a code of prohibitions, rather than believe, with St Augustine of Hippo, that the Christian has only one relevant injunction, 'love God and do what you like'. The ethic of the second-mile is both more exacting and more exhilarating, and it does not appeal to cautious souls. Thus, from the earliest days, legalism has always fought against the life of the Spirit. The other persistently-recurring element of Judaism within Christianity has been millenarianism, and, moreover, one more material than spiritual in its allocation of rewards to the faithful.

The Judaistic tendencies within the movements claiming to be fully Christian are: Seventh-Day Adventism, Jehovah's Witnesses, British-Israel and Mormonism. Seventh-Day Adventism revives sabbatarianism, making it a doctrine essential for salvation, and in its millenarianism limits the number of the elect to its own members. The Jehovah's Witnesses develop their doctrine of soul-sleep and their millenarianism on an Old Testament foundation. They also circumscribe salvation by limiting it to their own communion. The British-Israelites have reduced the doctrine of election to favouritism and their God to an Anglo-Saxon tribal deity. The patriarchial ethics and the apocalypticism of Mormonism reflects a Judaistic, rather than a Christian, colouring. The success of these Judaistic revisions of Christianity forces on Christians the question: What home truths have these sects to teach the Churches? These lessons appear to be three. Firstly, their adherents have a knowledge of the contents of the Holy Scriptures which Christians would do well to emulate. The Bible is the record of the revelation of the mighty acts of God consummated in the life, death, resurrection and ascension of Jesus Christ, and the donation of the Holy Spirit; it is the supreme witness to the origin of our faith, and trust in Christ as the contemporary Lord is recreated and nourished by it. For this reason alone it is imperative that Christians should become again the people of the

Book. The very facility with which adherents of Judaistic sects cite chapter and verse of the Scriptures and the enthusiasm with which Communists con their 'Red Bible', *Das Kapital* of Karl Marx, should drive Christians back to the Word as their iron-rations and marching orders.

But that is not enough, for clearly a thorough knowledge of the Bible has not prevented the new movements from being heretical. In the second place, what is required is a *critical* knowledge of the Holy Writ. Biblicism becomes heretical because it has no standard of reference by which to evaluate the different parts of the Scriptures. Claiming to believe that the Bible is equally inspired in all its parts, it nevertheless builds on private interpretation of a selection of the Law and of the Apocalyptic parts of Scripture. The only adequate criterion is 'the mind of Christ' by which Christians understand the life of our Lord as recorded in those superb biographies, the Gospels, and in the leading of the Holy Spirit given to the Apostles and recorded in the other books of the New Testament. This standard disenthralls the Christian from the authority of the Old Dispensation and translates him 'into the kingdom of the love of God's dear Son'. For 'the Law came by Moses, but grace and truth by Christ'. His ethical motivation is the constraint of the love of Christ. The morality of justice under the Old Dispensation is replaced by the profounder understanding of forgiveness which is, according to Dr Reinhold Niebuhr, 'the crown of Christian ethics'. Whatever in the Old Covenant is contrary to the attitude or the acts of Christ is un-Christian or sub-Christian, and therefore of no authority for the Christian man. In particular, a critical understanding of the Scriptures liberates the Christian from regarding prophetical and apocalyptic books as cryptograms from which the ingenious Bibliolater may predict the future in detail.

The success of these movements should, in fact, force the Christian Church to attempt a thorough revaluation not only of the Bible, but of the Holy Spirit and of the Church itself as the source of authority for Christian doctrine. History has shown that the Bible of itself, when regarded as infallible and equally inspired in all its parts, leads to the formation of heretical sects. It also shows that an exclusive dependence upon the Holy Spirit leads to such aberrations as characterized the fantastic 'rule of the saints' in the days of the Commonwealth in England, when every man claimed his idiosyncrasies as new revelations; and that exclusive dependence upon the Church as the organ of truth leads to the propounding of unbiblical doctrines, such as the Assumption of the Blessed Virgin and the Immaculate Conception, as of the essence of the faith. The Bible, the Church, and the individual inspired by the Holy Spirit are three interlocking authorities for the Christian faith. It is clear that the Bible is of primary, the Church of secondary, and the inspired individual of tertiary importance. The new movements have at least helped the Church to reconsider the problem of authority. The groups may be thanked for this at least, that they are forcing the contemporary Church to realize its urgency.

In the third place, the 'Judaistic' heretics have an enthusiasm in communicating their erratic tenets which Christians would do well to emulate in the spreading of the truth as it is in Christ Jesus. As instances of this we may take the remarkable organization of the Jehovah's Witnesses which obliges each of their members to canvass every householder in the interests of their doctrines, so much so that they have become a by-word for importunity and pertinacity, and the missionary zeal of the Seventh-Day Adventists and Mormons who have a reputation second only to the Moravians for the high proportion of their adherents who become missionaries in all parts of the earth. The warning of Professor J. R. Coates is timely:

> The success of heresies and unorthodox cults is a measure of the failure of the Church. As with Spiritualism, Christian Science, and Adventism, so with British-Israel: its propagandists minister to real human needs, and its plausibility is largely due to its ingenuity in relating the Bible to contemporary experience and to current affairs.[1]

I I

Several other cults brought under review belong to the Gnostic type of heresy. They represent attempts to combine elements of Christian teaching with doctrines of other systems or faiths. The early Christians had to counter not only a

[1] *Expository Times*, Vol. LIV, p. 313.

Judaizing tendency but also a Hellenistic movement. Dr Radford rightly explains the attractions of such eclecticism as due

> partly to the desire to combine non-Christian ideas with Christian ideas, or to winning outsiders by going as near as possible to their position, and in still larger part to the wish of thinking men to understand and explain the Christian faith for thinking men.[1]

Many philosophers have attempted to find a common religion which summed up the spiritual values of all religions from the days of Lord Herbert of Cherbury to our contemporary, Professor Hocking of Harvard. To them doctrine was the ineffectual attempt of the different religions to capture in words the ineffable experiences of the mystics and the moralists. They argued that it ought to be possible to express the same experiences in common concepts. The renewed impetus to provide a common religion for humanity derives partly from the comparative study of religion, partly from the conviction that it is better for an increasingly secular civilization to have one religion rather than none, and partly from a desire to end nationalism and internecine warfare by acknowledging an overarching loyalty to one authoritative creed. Whilst several religions have been considered for the honour of being acclaimed the universal religion of mankind, the Christian faith has been found wanting by philosophers both because of its claim for finality and for its 'scandal of particularity'. Christians have stubbornly refused to allow their Saviour to consort on terms of equality in their estimation with Confucius, the Buddha, or Mohammed, the 'seal of the prophets'. Thus their claim that the Incarnation of the eternal Son of God is the final revelation of the nature and activity of God makes them unable to relegate the Christ to a convenient Pantheon in which all religious teachers are worshipped alike. The anchor of their faith in history, as recorded in the saga of the mighty acts of God, means that Christianity cannot be reduced to a philosophy.

Examples of the Gnostic type of heresy are Theosophy, Spiritism, and Christian Science. Its adherents are often former Christians. Of contemporary Gnosticism, Dr Radford says:

[1] *Ancient Heresies in Modern Dress*, p. 34.

The creed by which the Christian Scientist explains the facts of faith-healing is a latter-day Gnosticism which denies not merely the spiritual possibilities of the material world but also its reality as an object of experience. Theosophy is a latter-day Gnosticism which dissolves the Gospel into an allegory, fills the spiritual world with the creations of Hindu fancy, and now is summoning Christendom and all other religions to look to the East for another reincarnation of the Christ-spirit as the world teacher who is to inaugurate a new world-faith.[1]

We may note that Gnostic eclecticisms have the following features in common. Their religion appeals to the proud rather than the humble in heart, for it claims to sum up the best in other religions and thus castigates adherents of the older faiths as old-fashioned. Its appeal is largely to intellectuals and initiates and not to the great under-privileged multitudes of the world. Their philosophy is almost always pantheistic and shares the characteristic weaknesses of that outlook; for example, it despises the body which for the Christian is the temple of the Holy Spirit; it teaches an automatic immortality which makes an end of a moral interpretation of history; it depersonalizes God so that he becomes an 'essence' or a 'principle' and ceases to be *the* Person; consequently it despises history and the world as illusory, and shows an ostrich-like optimism towards sin, and an unwillingness to change the social conditions, which militate against the full development of personality-in-community. Salvation is through identification with God by means of mediation, not by the transformation of the will.

The criticism of any attempt to find a common religion such as Theosophy is that no religion can be successful which builds only upon the highest common factors in all religions. The history of eighteenth-century Deism in England, with its attempt to banish distinctive doctrines in the interests of a religion that could be accepted by all men of good sense, proves that the resulting creed was ineffectual in the attempt to transform the lives of men. John Howe rightly parodied it as affirming, 'There shall be a God, provided he be not meddlesome'. Furthermore, the different religions do not mix, because they teach different, not common, tenets. Christianity is both world-

Ancient Heresies in Modern Dress, p. 34.

affirming and world-denying. Buddhism is entirely world-denying. Christianity affirms that God the father is Creator and Controller of the universe. Buddhism denies the existence of a personal God at all. Yet it is mainly these two religions which Theosophy has tried to combine.

The mistake of Spiritism and Christian Science, which have closer affinities with the Christian Faith, is to attempt to make one Christian tenet into the whole of Christianity. Although Professor Bethune-Baker was writing of early heresiarchs, his explanation of the motivation of heresy is applicable to both Spiritism and Christian Science. He declares that heterodoxy arose:

> when they seized on a few facts as though they were all the facts, and from these few framed theories to explain and interpret all; when they put forward a meagre and immature conception as a full-grown representation of the Christian idea of life.[1]

In each case the success of these two cults has been due to the failure of the Church to keep in the forefront of its teaching the truths which they seceded to maintain. The Spiritists have reaffirmed the centrality of the doctrine of the Resurrection in the Christian faith, and have taken the belief in the Communion of Saints as the centre and sum of their faith. The Christian Scientists have seen the overwhelming importance of faith in the New Testament narratives and applied it to the sicknesses of humanity. In fact, both the doctrine of the Communion of Saints and the practice of faith-healing are important constituents of the Christian faith and life. These needed to be reaffirmed, but the mistake of the heretics was to assert that these comprehended the entire faith.

It has been already remarked that Gnostic heresies find the readiest converts amongst weak Christians. This provides an obvious lesson for the historic Churches. Their candidates for confirmation or membership must be instructed in the biblical faith as summarized in the Apostles' Creed, in Christian conduct as summarized in the Decalogue and the Beatitudes, and in Christian devotions as summarized in the Lord's Prayer. A

[1] *An Introduction to the Early History of Christian Doctrine* (Methuen, 1938), pp. 4-5.

thorough understanding of these is a minimal necessity for every Christian.

A further curious factor in modern heresies which deserves the attention of the Churches is the important part played by women in their foundation and continuance. It is surely significant that the two founders of Theosophy were Madame Blavatsky and Mrs Annie Besant, that Christian Science owes its origin to Mrs Mary Baker Eddy, and that the originator of Seventh-Day Adventism was Mrs Ellen White. It might be suggested that in each case men had pioneered the thought-forms of the new systems, but none the less the success of these cults is due to the drive of energetic women. Can this fact have any significance for the Churches? One reason for the interest of women in these new faiths is that their place is recognized in their hierarchies, as it is not in the historic Christian Churches. Although Christians have affirmed for almost twenty centuries with St Paul that 'there is neither male nor female, but all are one in Christ Jesus', this belief rarely results in the ordination of women, far less in their elevation to a high place in the government of the Christian Church. Only a small number of women ministers exist in the Protestant Churches; as yet the Roman Catholic, the Orthodox and Anglican Churches do not admit women to the priesthood. The Society of Friends does not ordain either men or women, but both sexes have equal rights and privileges. If all the Churches were to remove this form of sexual discrimination, the temptation for devout women to set up their own forms of cults, or to gravitate towards those sects that accord women a higher status, would be greatly reduced. Furthermore, it seems that the heretical cults founded by women show a warmth of fellowship that is so often unwarrantably absent in the historic Churches. The same warmth partly accounts for the success of the Moral Re-Armament movement.

III

Is it possible to catalogue the tendencies of the new movements in such a way as to underline their strength and weakness? The attempt will be made to summarize those factors which two or three of them hold in common. These may serve as useful danger signals to the members of both the new movements and the historic Churches.

There is the danger of mistaking the part for the whole in Christian faith or practice. Two examples are Christian Science and Theosophy.

There is the danger of an over-emphasis on the Old Testament to the detriment of the New. Examples of this tendency are Jehovah's Witnesses, Seventh-Day Adventism, Christadelphianism, Mormonism, and British-Israel.

There is the danger of confusing Christianity with Pantheism. Both Theosophy and Christian Science are examples of this confusion.

There is the danger of seeking for greater assurance in the religious life than faith in Christ offers. Spiritism, with its attempt to obtain experimental proof of life after death, is one example, and the predictions of the Millenarian groups provide another. Each is a product of scepticism rather than of trust.

There is the danger of spiritual pride which issues in the schism of a 'holier-than-thou' attitude, or in the formation of an esoteric cult for initiates or intellectuals only. Diverse examples of this characteristic are found in Moral Rearmament, Theosophy, and some of the Millenarian groups. The corrective is the charity of the One Holy Catholic and Apostolic Church, of which the historic Communions are branches, honouring individuals of all races and classes and types.

There is the danger of using God as a means to an end. This is the case when God is a convenience for obtaining excellent health in Christian Science, or as a means of obtaining political leadership of the world as in British-Israel, or as the supreme weapon in defeating Communism as conceived by the M.R.A.

There is the danger of individualistic pietism, quietism, and a concentration on 'glory for me'. Its correlative is the renunciation of many civic and political responsibilities, and is evinced by Theosophists, Jehovah's Witnesses, Christian Scientists and Seventh-Day Adventists. It also contributed to the success of Marxism by causing the latter to condemn Christianity as 'dope'.

There is the supreme danger of failing to acknowledge the fullness, the uniqueness and the finality of the Christian doctrine of the Incarnation. Nearly all groups suffer from this defect, otherwise they would not have come into being. Where Jesus is thought of as a first-century teacher and inspired prophet, as was often the case in communions which accepted what was known as a 'reduced Christology', the way was already open for the displacement of Jesus by later and self-appointed prophets like Ellen White, Mary Baker Eddy, Joseph Smith or Annie Besant. Where he is accepted as the Eternal and only-begotten Son of God, and worshipped as the Lord of lords and King of kings, and obeyed as Master, Christian humility makes it unlikely for a mere human to pretend to a better insight into the mind of God than Jesus had.

IV

'Mainstream' Christianity will be most attractive when it is most true to its own inheritance. If it cares for the bodies, the souls, and the organization of a just order of society, it will have nothing to fear from Communism. If the fellowship of Christians is a genuine community and family springing from their communion with the God and Father of us all, if Christian members confess their sins in sincerity and with a desire to make reparation to those whom they have wronged, and if they provide a way of life with opportunities of thrilling service for its younger members, historic Christianity can dispense with Moral Re-Armament's services. If it places the doctrines of the resurrection and of the Communion of Saints in the centre of its worship, the spurious attractions of Spiritism will be unavailing because dispelled by faith in the Risen Christ. If Christianity takes seriously the miraculous powers of faith in a wonder-working God, Christian Science will lose its attractions. If Christians really believe that their Lord has won a triple victory over sin, suffering and death, and that 'all things work together for good to them that love God', they will not relapse into the superstition of Astrology. If the Churches proclaim of Christ by life and by lip that 'there is none other Name whereby we must be saved', Theosophy will lose its enchantments. If the Church by its abounding charity manifests in its international and interracial fellowship that there is neither 'Jew nor Greek, bond nor free', and that God is no respecter of persons, all racialistic distortions of the faith such as British-Israel will earn the unceasing antagonism of Christians. If Christians accept the general promises of Christ, and do not try to implement his reverent silences with details drawn from their own materialistic imaginations, and show a comparable zeal for transmitting their holy faith, then the unseemly predictions of the Seventh-Day Adventists and Jehovah's Witnesses will lose their interest.

In the last analysis, however, there must be a radical change in the approach of the historic Churches to these new movements. Clarity must be supplemented with charity.

12

EPILOGUE: THE WAY OF ENCOUNTER

Speaking the truth in love. (Eph. 4.15)

HOWEVER sympathetically we have tried to look at the new spiritual movements hitherto, we have necessarily observed them from the *outside*. In so doing, it is inevitable that we should have stressed the differences between them and the historic Christian churches. This Epilogue will emphasize the important possibilities latent in a more positive approach of personal and group encounter with a view to *inside* appreciation and understanding. The relations between Roman Catholics, Orthodox, Anglicans and Protestants are closer at present than they have ever been before. It is essential that there should be a determined attempt to draw together the historic Christian Churches and the spiritual movements, especially those of a Christian intention among the latter. Taking the whole spectrum of movements discussed in this book, it is clear that encounter will be welcomed by some, unwelcome to others, and probably a matter of sheer indifference to yet others.

In this situation it is important to try to do three things. First, we must attempt to discern those signs by which a movement is developing into a denomination, and particularly a denomination that seeks closer association with the historic Christian Churches. For convenience, we shall describe the movement towards the centre of the historic churches as *centripetal*, and the movement away from the centre as *centrifugal*. We are, then, looking for signs of change from a centrifugal to a centripetal direction. Secondly, we must identify those movements which are clearly centripetal. Thirdly, by a new attitude on our part, and by actions clearly reflecting that attitude, we must encourage and accelerate the centripetal movement.

I

What signs mark the change in direction from hostility to growing appreciation of the historic churches on the part of new spiritual movements?

(1) *Social approximation.* Throughout these pages it has been urged that there are social as well as theological factors accounting for the original hostility and mutual suspicion. By the same token when social differences between the older denominations and newer movements lessen, a mutual appreciation becomes possible. As we shall see later, it does not inevitably follow that social approximation leads to theological approximation, but it removes an important ground of misunderstanding.

In the increased prosperity of modern America, as in the British welfare-state, there is a higher common level of education and a higher appreciation of culture. The 'disinherited' groups are coming into their inheritance. (And about time, too!) In consequence, 'side-stream' Christians increasingly wear clothes and use vocabularies indistinguishable from 'main-stream' Christians. 'Store-front' churches in the U.S.A. move into suburban areas and comply with the municipal building requirements. 'Tin tabernacles' in the U.K. yield to brick structures. Thus, apart from the names on the noticeboards, the churches of certain of the new movements are no different from the neo-Gothic of the Methodist church on High Street or the neo-colonial United Church of Christ or the cantilevered sanctuaries of the new Roman Catholic or Episcopal churches on Main Street.

These Christians have arrived socially, and the older churches should hang out the flags, instead of muttering as they so often do. As long as the society is open-ended, even if the parents don't quite arrive, their children will. Thus, the social basis for suspicion is disintegrating.

This mixing process is speedier in America than in Britain, because of the great mobility of population in the States, where on an average one family in four changes its home each year.

There are endless natural opportunities for dialogue in parents-and-teachers' associations, professional and trade gatherings and socials, and in factories, shops and offices. One hopes that unofficial dialogue will lead to official conversations.

(2) *The maturation of the second and third generations.* The enthusiasm of first generation Bible-based movements is notoriously difficult to preserve in the second and third generations. Success brings in numbers, and numbers require a complex organization. Inevitably the close-knit fellowship of the pioneers, despite the organization of gigantic conventions, leads to a remoteness from the grass roots. The increasingly complex organization at regional and national levels, is further complicated by the need for specialists and institutions where evangelistic, social, educational, and medical training may be provided. Relationships tend to become less spontaneous and more formal.

(3) As a result of the changes induced by the first and second factors, a third emerges. It is the *demand for a more educated ministry and a more predictable form of worship.*

Bible Institutes are admirable for training evangelists, but are not sophisticated enough for training ministers. Thus colleges and seminaries are founded. But if these institutions are to receive accreditation in the United States their teachers (at least a high proportion of them) must have doctoral degrees. Hence the reason for the most able and ambitious teachers and ministers attending the Graduate Schools of the large universities or university-related interdenominational seminaries, such as Harvard or Yale Divinity School or Union Seminary in New York City in the East, or Chicago Divinity School in the mid-West, or the new Graduate Union of Seminaries at Berkeley in the far West.

The results can be imagined. In the free encounter such institutions provide, the representatives of the new movements contribute to the fracturing of stereotypes and prejudices. Personal friendships are made that cut across denominational frontiers. Many labels are found to be merely libels. An inevitable ecumenical chain-reaction ensues as a Presbyterian makes a life-long friend of a Pentecostalist or a Northern Baptist sees that a Seventh-Day Adventist is a comrade, not a competitor. All members of such an interdenominational seminary are responsible for conducting prayers, and there is at first hostility to and later a growing appreciation of the possibility of supplementing forms of prayer with free prayers, and a heightened appreciation of what the sacramental life means to Lutherans and Anglicans, for example. Slowly but surely, a more sophisticated theology emerges in the preaching and greater order and dignity in the conduct of divine worship.

(4) *Changes in theology and the Christian life.* The other changes we have marked also produce subtle transformations of emphasis in Christian belief and behaviour. Christianity is now recognized to be world-affirming as well as world-denying. As a result there is less emphasis on the immediacy of the Second Coming of Christ. The hope is not denied; it is delayed. There is less interest in the possible predictions of the Apocalypse.

There is a growing embarrassment about motor-mechanisms as proofs of the dynamic endowment of the Holy Spirit. The sensitive leader of the American Pentecostalists, David J. du Plessis, declares: 'Let me say right here that I consider it heresy to speak of shaking, trembling, falling, dancing, clapping, shouting and such actions as manifestations of the Holy Spirit. They are purely human reactions to the power of the Holy Spirit.'[1] Du Plessis fully recognizes the need to move from the nursery stage of Christianity to adulthood, but he will not forbid these joyous expressions of the first careless rapture of converts.

There are also likely to be changes in ethical patterns. These will probably include a deeper involvement in citizenship and community affairs, and a recognition that moral issues are rarely a choice between divine or diabolical alternatives. An original simplistic legalism will be transformed by the growing complexity of the involved life, by the need to make due allowances for different temperaments and circumstances, and, in short, the need to be more compassionate and less expulsive in church discipline.

(5) The most important sign of all is *an increase in charity*

---

[1] A citation from *The Spirit Bade Me Go* (published by the author at 3742 Linwood Avenue, Oakland, California, 1963), contained in an impressive review of the book by Bishop Lesslie Newbigin in *Frontier*, Summer issue, 1964, pp. 144-5.

to other religious groups. (And who dares to say that the historic Christian churches are filled with charity and compassion?) This achievement (more properly an endowment) will be symbolized by the desire to issue—on the side of the older denominations—and to accept—on the side of the newer movements—invitations to join ministerial fraternals, and the Evangelical Alliance. The centripetal movement will have gained great momentum when some of these movements have been welcomed into the comity of the World Council of Churches, the non-Roman Catholic instrument and expression of ecumenism.

I I

Which of the new movements we have considered show these signs of centripetal movement, and which show the opposite centrifugal signs?

Of all the new movements the nearest to the historic Christian churches is the Pentecostalist. It is the most rapidly growing evangelical expression of contemporary Christianity. It has the marks of a denomination, or series of associated denominations, in its social composition (without the loss of vigour), its organizational complexity, its institutions for educational, theological and medical training, and in a growing sophistication and maturity. Its increasing charity has resulted in its membership of the Evangelical Alliance. It has even been awarded the ultimate recognition in respectability (I write ironically) in the occasional broadcast of its large gatherings in England by the British Broadcasting Corporation. It has still to be brought into the World Council of Churches, where it almost certainly belongs as Protestantism's most successful missionary arm in Latin America and other areas. Its very dynamism could make the historic churches jealous of it, or it could become contemptuous of the static state of the historic churches. It has, in fact, not succumbed to the latter temptation and its leaders, at least, are exceedingly open in their dialogue with leaders of the 'mainline' churches. If the historic churches have still questions to be asked about 'tongues', the Pentecostalists may have more radical questions to ask about the nature of Christian witness and of how the Gospel is demonstrated with power to the outsider.

The centripetal movement is also shown, though to a lesser degree, by the Seventh-Day Adventists and associated groups. They, too, are a Christian missionary organization with international ramifications and unbounded zeal. They are engaged in medical, educational, social, and evangelistic work that compels admiration. There is, however, still sufficient difference between them and the historic churches (in the observance of the seventh day and in their re-interpretation of the doctrine of the Atonement) to put a brake on the predominantly centripetal movement. In the case of the Pentecostalists high-level dialogue is in progress; in the case of the Seventh-Day Adventists, it ought to begin as the prelude to better understanding.

Moral Re-armament is both related to and independent from the historic churches. Many of its members are also members of the churches. Many others are not. For some it is a supplement of the work of the Church; for others it is a moral and spiritual substitute for the Church. It arose from the historic churches, Lutheran and Anglican. Conceivably, if it were so to choose, it might be re-incorporated in the Church. At present, however, it moves parallel to the Church and is able to attract those who are beyond the immediate reach of the Church. Its independence gives it great freedom for experimentation, but equally, as has been argued, it has lost some of the ballast and depth of tradition. Certainly it does not seem to be hostile to the historic churches, nor (however glad it is to get the support of individual churchmen) does it seem particularly friendly to denominations as denominations. It is an ideology and should not therefore be regarded as other than supplementing the ethical ideals of Christianity. It could develop a centripetal movement.

The Mormons, or the Church of Jesus Christ of Latter-Day saints, suggest a possibility of fruitful encounter with the 'main-stream' churches from their name, their missionary zeal and international extension, their social 'spread', and their acknowledgment of the Bible's importance. To this extent they seem to be a centripetal movement. Other characteristics of theirs propel them in a centrifugal direction. The most important factor in this regard is their supplementation of the Bible with the *Book of Mormon, Doctrine and Covenants*, and the *Pearl of Great Price.*[1] God is said in the first of these books to admit the incompleteness of earlier revelation in the Old and New Testaments thus: 'Thou fool, that shall say: A Bible. we have got a Bible, and we need no more Bible. . . . Wherefore, because that ye have a Bible, ye need not suppose that it contains all my words; neither need ye suppose that I have not caused more to be written.'[2] It is the post-Biblical 'revelations' that create the greatest difficulties in the way of an encounter, as in the case of Christian Science. But it is always possible, however unlikely at present, that later revelations from the Presidents of the Mormons may encourage a return to the acceptance of the primacy of the original Bible.

In theory, Jehovah's Witnesses, as a biblically-based movement, ought to be moving towards the historic churches. In fact, it is centrifugal and as anti-ecclesiastical as any religious movement could be. It is an immensely courageous and a formidably cohesive movement. It is so cohesive and so autocratically controlled that it does not, at least for the present, seem open to encounter. This is partly because its members are predominantly still socially disinherited and have every reason for being suspicious of the well-to-do. It is partly that their cohesion consists in being united in the belief that all other religious groups are wholly in the wrong and they are wholly in the right. It is also partly due to the inflexible power of their leadership. Perhaps it is most of all due to their understanding of God (at least as it appears on the outside) which seems to be a combination of militancy to the many and mercy to the very few. One has sadly to conclude that any real encounter is almost impossible.

British-Israel is an ideology held by certain conservative Christians in the English-speaking part of the world, and not a separate religious organization complete with separate creed, rites and ceremonies. It is only one significant example of a nationalistic and racialistic distortion which misrepresents the universalistic implications of Christ's Gospel. Many other

[1] It should be noted that the *Pearl* contains the 'Book of Moses' from the 'Inspired Bible' of Joseph Smith, of which the first and seventh chapters are significant additions and modifications of the first six chapters of Genesis.

[2] See the *Book of Mormon*, II Nephi, 29:6ff.

Christians in many denominations are also distorted by racial prejudices of a similar kind, though not articulated so thoroughly or disseminated so openly. These, whether British-Israelites or the more vehement and cruel Klu Klux Klan, are indisputably the 'foes of our own household'. (These are vision-blocking splinters in the eyes of the historic churches which should prevent the churchly kettles from calling new movements black pots.)

Many factors might be the grounds of hope for a happy encounter between Christian Science and the Ecumenical Movement. These would include: the 'Christian' in the title, the requirement of regular public and private readings from the Bible, and a great renewal of interest in faith-healing on the part of many of the historic churches. Moreover, the Christian Scientists are a cheerful and helpful cross-section of the middle and upper-middle classes. Furthermore, one of their chaplains was linked with three others in death while saving lives on a torpedoed ship during World War II and is commemorated in the Four Chaplains Window of the chapel of Boston University. The real barrier is that the Bible is supplemented by a secondary source of revelation, *Science and Health*, which is the authoritative 'key' to unlock the Scriptures. Moreover, that volume, however many its genuine spiritual insights are, is a compound of American transcendentalism and Oriental immateriality which cannot be squared with the religion of the Incarnation. Change is not likely while the Board of Trustees are motivated by an inflexible archaism. Thus socially there is a centripetal movement, and ideologically there is a centrifugal movement. Any genuine encounter looks exceedingly improbable for the immediate future.

Theosophy is a very sophisticated amalgam of the philosophies of several religions, while Spiritism (apart from the Society for Psychical Research) is a relatively unsophisticated attempt to make contact with the survivors of death in a spirit-world. Though they are placed together in this single paragraph, they differ radically in method, as in intellectual and emotional appeal. Both represent in a technocratic and materialistic world a spiritual alternative to materialism. Neither is in fact or intention Christian, though both combine some Christian with non-Christian elements of doctrine. Since they are not Christian, they cannot be 'deviations', They are alternatives competing for human allegiance in this chaotic century.

It will be clear then that the likeliest immediate encounters will take place within those new spiritual movements which approximate to Protestantism in the primacy accorded to the Bible over tradition.

III

But what attitudes and actions on the part of individuals or groups within the historic churches are like to encourage the centripetal movements?

It is abundantly clear that an essential preparation for the new encounter will be a *new attitude*. On our side of the divide there must be a new openness and a new humility. It can be helped by the recalling of some crucial facts and convictions.

We can begin by recognizing (as I have tried to do in earlier chapters) the great strengths of all these movements which have won them convinced adherents. It is clear that these values will be best expounded by those holding them rather than by the most sympathetic outside observer.

Then we might reflect that many of our so-called 'historic churches' were regarded by the 'more historic churches' as interlopers and schismatics when they originated. This is true of the Baptists and Congregationalists in the sixteenth century (as of the earlier Lutherans and Presbyterians of the same century) and of the Methodists of the eighteenth century. These denominations were originally even hostile to one another. Now the historic churches are seen to be the allies of the more historic churches, and it is desirable that we should anticipate the judgment of history in the case of the new movements.

A very sobering fact is that all Christendom is in fact in schism. It is true that most denominations are unhappy to remain as 'separated brethren', but separated they are. So are the members of the new movements that are Christian in intention. We are all members of the same convoy of Christians traversing the stormy waters of the present. Even if we interpret the Commander-in-chief's signals with some differences, we none of us intend to flout his authority. Or, to be more precise, we debate about how faithfully some of the captains have relayed the orders.

We should also consider that the purpose of an encounter is to give freely of our convictions and of our doubts and to receive the same. We may pride ourselves on our church order as if it were part of the very Gospel itself, but it may be the result of absolutizing the finite and confounding our preferences with the Divine will for all men. We may rightly treasure our catholicity (in the sense of the wealth of guidance we inherit from many centuries and saints and their devotional, sacramental, and ethical practice). We may be rightly grateful for the rich heritage of a Christian culture in music, art, and architecture. But this inheritance is to be spent, given away, not hoarded, and our new friends have need of it as we did. Their ardour and vital experimentation in witness is what they have to give to us. It is only in encounter that we shall learn what gifts have to be exchanged and what confessions and reparations must be made.

Supremely, we and they need together to learn the art of speaking and acting the truth in love. This cannot be done without deep and continuing mutual involvement on the part of the older and the newer denominations. If the danger in the past has been speaking the truth dogmatically (as if it were our truth and not God's), the danger of the present could be that we speak not lovingly but sentimentally and achieve only a relationship of cordial ambiguity. Thus we would fall a prey to doctrinal relativism. (I do not forget that Chesterton remarked that the effect of studying comparative religions was to make one only comparatively religious!)

We are more likely to attain that attitude of speaking and acting the truth in love if we recollect that it was as the compassionate Servant of God that our Lord won his way into the hearts of men, and that he forbade his disciples to lord it over others, but to serve them.

Above all we should constantly remember that our Lord has sheep 'not of this fold' who hear his voice and that *he* knows his own. We believe that he will ultimately bring them into one fold, and it is not our job to erect barbed wire fences of suspicion and hostility, but to demolish them. If we—on the side of the historic Christian Churches—are ever inclined to think God's other charges are black sheep or worse, sheep in wolves' clothing—the terrible darkening of the inner eye that Pharisaism produces—then we must look to the wolf within us. We all need the grace which God in Christ bestows undeservingly on each. This is the best spirit in which to work for *rapprochement*.

But holy attitudes must be expressed in holy actions. And perhaps the holiest are those which are done without hope of earthly fruit. If that be so, we must not consider the most improbable encounter fruitless. But it is good Christian strategy also to concentrate on the most probable objectives. These actions in which we engage as individuals or as members of groups will demand an overcoming of suspicion by an honest and cordial meeting of minds and hearts. Each reader will have his or her own ideas how to improve the contacts which every day or every week brings for the work of reconciliation. It would be impertinent for the author to try to tell, if he could, how keen individuals will find the way.

But, apart from the important individual meetings for dialogue, there must be opportunities for a more official but no less friendly encounter. Young people's groups in local churches could arrange to meet their opposite numbers in the new movements. Local churches or delegations from them could arrange for exchanges of preaching and worship. Local clergy and ministers could invite local leaders of the new movements to join their fraternal if the good feeling were to be reciprocated. And there is the great need for such action at denominational levels.

For long the Anglican and Lutheran Communions have acted as 'bridge-churches' because of their strategic position straddling the division between Catholicism and Protestantism. It is conceivable that the Methodist and Baptist Communions could be bridge-churches between the Anglicans and Lutherans on the one hand and the new movements on the other.

Catholic-Protestant dialogue is in full swing. The need for a dialogue between Protestantism and the new spiritual movements on the left-wing is already overdue.

INDEX

INDEX